Advance Reviews
for *Choosing Peace*

"Clear, thoughtful, important, this book invites you to reconsider the way you move through the world. Accept the invitation, welcome the work, engage the process, it has great potential to transform your life."

—**Valerie Rose Belanger**,
Managing Director, Yale World Fellows, Yale University

"Read it. Practice it. Live it. Practical and poignant, *Choosing Peace* offers a storehouse of tools for making life more satisfying emotionally and concretely. Filled with stories that inspire and chapters that teach a new way to be in the world, getting what you want and giving to others takes on a whole new level of relationship and do-ability. For home or business, this book could change the way you interact forever. We're recommending it to our business and nonprofit clients!"

—**Gregg Kendrick**,
Speaker, Consultant, Workplace Mediator, and Certified Trainer - Center for Nonviolent Communication and IC Globally Team Member at Basileia, LLC

—**Marie Miyashiro**,
Author of *The Empathy Factor* and Workplace Consultant, Leadership and Whole System Facilitator, Speaker and IC Globally Team Member at Elucity Network, Inc.

"John Kinyon and Ike Lasater's book, *Choosing Peace: New Ways to Communicate to Reduce Stress, Create Connection, and Resolve Conflict*, is a fresh approach to meeting conflict with an eye on peaceful resolution; and, how doing this changes *everything* for *everyone* involved. Their blending of the Nonviolent Communication model and traditional mediation practices offers a process to cut through anger, resentment and miscommunications—thus, setting the foundation for inner peace and peace in our relationships. No kidding. It's like magic—so clear and simple and transformative."

—**Mary Mackenzie**,
Author, *Peaceful Living: Daily Meditations for Living with Love, Healing and Compassion*; Co-founder, NVC Academy; Executive Director, Peace Workshop, International; Certified Nonviolent Communication Trainer; Mediator

"The warmth, wisdom and clarity of the authors clearly comes across in this book. I really enjoy how they make conflict a normal everyday thing that happens to all of us, and suggest that we can learn how to handle conflict rather than seeing it as a sign that something is wrong. Use Ike and John's way of dealing with conflict to harvest the means to achieve internal and external peace."

—**Liv Larsson**,
Mediator and author of *A Helping Hand, Mediation with Nonviolent Communication and Anger, Guilt and Shame—Reclaiming Power and Choice.*

"Gandhi said, 'In a gentle way you can shake the world.' *Choosing Peace* offers radical, yet practical instruction to do just that. Don't merely read this book. Practice the wisdom you discover in it to harness the transformative power of choice that resides within every conflict. You will be astonished."

—**Christine Flaherty**,
Healthcare Executive, CNVC Certified Trainer

"I used to avoid conflict at all costs and consequently would sometimes not be able to live my deepest values of telling the truth and living an authentic life. Through trainings with Ike and John I learned precious and valuable techniques for staying present with people no matter what they have to say. Now, I not only tolerate conflict better but am even excited to be in situations of conflict because I have learned that they can often lead to deeper honesty and connection. I am happy to recommend this clear, practical and deeply inspiring book so that even more people can learn these ways of being that our world so sorely needs."

—**Marcia Miller**,
Owner, Yoga On High

"John and Ike take Marshall Rosenberg's work to a whole new level—they have unpacked the components of NVC and placed them into small understandable nourishing bites, incorporated the fight-flight-freeze dynamic, offered an invitation to practice these skills throughout the book and intertwined from beginning to end, they offer exciting real-life examples highlighting a cast of characters as they learn, grow and practice the skills and techniques of Mediate Your Life. A powerful book that will have you waiting anxiously for the next in their series to be published."

—**Sylvia Haskvitz, MA, RD**,
Author of *Eat by Choice, Not by Habit*

"*Choosing Peace* is a remarkable contribution to the world of mediation and peacemaking. The book is both eminently practical—how do I convey what is going on in me clearly and without offense?—and deeply inspiring—how can I use my new understanding to create a harmonious world? The writing is crisp and the stories compelling. Most of all, Ike and John have reduced the complexity of peacemaking to the comprehensible—not an easy take. I have been a full-time mediator for more than decade, and have helped many hundreds find peace and resolution. I would credit Ike and John above all others in offering me the intellectual understandings and the practical tools necessary to make this a reality. *Choosing Peace* is simply a continuation of their outstanding work. I hope the whole world reads it."

—**Larry Rosen,**
Attorney-mediator, founder of Through Understanding

"Ike and John write with open hearts about the purpose of NVC. In a motivating way, they break down the components of NVC and highlight them with real-life examples. This clear step-by-step structure makes it easy to understand how to apply NVC in various settings. Follow what's in this book and you will be on your way to resolve conflicts in a deeply satisfying manner!"

—**Towe Widstrand,**
CNVC Certified Trainer, CNVC Assessor for Certification, Former CNVC Board Member and International Project Coordinator, Stockholm
http://towewidstrand.se

"*Choosing Peace* explains in simple, high-quality language the potential of Nonviolent Communication. I felt taken by the hand and, in a pleasant way, led through highlights of our daily communication pitfalls. With powerful imagery Ike and John succeed in drawing a picture of the theoretical model of NVC and bringing it within reach of everyone—whether new to NVC or already a skilled user. Beginners can get right to work and the more experienced practitioners can test their own insights or deepen them. Using recognizable family situations, the reader is introduced to the four basic steps of NVC and can therefore easily identify themselves with similar situations in their own personal or business environment. This makes the learning threshold very low. The unique approach in this book is a must for anyone interested in giving his own communication the necessary connectivity twist."

—**Harald Borjans**,
Owner of Daimoon BV, publisher of NVC-related books, the Netherlands
www.giraffendroom.nl

"The information in this book can change your life, as it did mine! After practicing the principles in this book I feel much more at ease with the way I handle myself in everyday life and in relation with others, which gives me both meaning and inspiration. I'm now applying these skills in my work life as well with amazing results, from coaching and educating organizations in soft skills, to helping prevent people from committing suicide in a chat support hot line. It takes some practice to learn these skills but believe me, it's worth it!"

—**Ola Tornberg**,
Trainer and soft skills specialist, Sweden

"In their book *Choosing Peace*, Ike Lasater and John Kinyon have brought a fresh approach to conflict, describing simple steps that lead first to a heart connection between the people involved, then to lasting solutions that work for everyone. The book gave me tools I now use every day, and showed me how to practice them until they became habits. Practicing is where the surprise came: I tried out these skills using my life's most mundane conflicts as material. Start simple and safe, right? I began noticing big shifts in how I was feeling, even without tackling any big issues. My relationships began to flow more smoothly. I am holding my temper more easily and feeling stressed less often. I've even started mediating between different aspects of myself. Now that I'm ending wars and settling scores within myself—choosing peace—I am finding that I like myself better and better each day."

—**Ed Niehaus**,
Chairman, Collaborative Drug Discovery, Inc.

"There is always the danger that communication could become a technique and become mechanical. But *Choosing Peace* is distilled from long and committed experience of mediating conflicts. The way it is presented through a story adds flesh and blood to the practice.

"'When you reach this shift in perspective, you do not let go of the stories or the judgments—they let go of you. The thoughts that were making you so miserable no longer have you in their grip.' Reminds us of the higher goals of the practice. The very title chosen for the book indicates something beyond lies tangled in the present messy sticky living. 'Practice Pause' is a useful device that keeps us at the same time glued to the practical aspects of the process.

"The authors have followed their initial inspiration that led them to Peshawar and guided them through long years of dedicated research and teaching of the process of choosing peace. I am confident that serious practice could lead the practitioners to a radical change."

—**Christlin Rajendram**,
Jesuit Priest, former Rector of Trincomalee Campus of Eastern University, Sri Lanka

Choosing Peace

New Ways to Communicate to Reduce Stress, Create Connection, and Resolve Conflict

Choosing Peace: New Ways to Communicate to Reduce Stress, Create Connection, and Resolve Conflict (Mediate Your Life: A Guide to Removing Barriers to Communication, Vol. 1)
by Ike Lasater & John Kinyon, with Julie Stiles and Mary Sitze

© 2014 Mediate Your Life, LLC

Mediate Your Life
P.O. Box 3539
Amherst, MA 01004

http://www.mediateyourlife.com
connect@mediateyourlife.com

ISBN-10: 0989972003
ISBN-13: 978-0-9899720-0-0

Table of Contents

Acknowledgements

We (Ike and John) want to express huge appreciation to our co-author Julie Stiles. We first began meeting in person, by phone and Skype with Julie in 2006. The three of us have worked steadily on the creation of this volume and the next six in the series. Julie has had the daunting challenge of taking our (Ike and John's) talking through the material of this book and turning it into clear, coherent, engaging, and accessible language for readers. She has at times needed to overcome a great deal of frustration and obstacles working with two characters such as us. For instance, we reorganized the project at least three times.

Julie brought a lot of her own valuable understanding and insights of this material into the writing, which has added significantly to the quality of the content. In fact, this book would not exist if it wasn't for Julie and her incredible patience, perseverance, and fortitude. We are grateful beyond what words can convey.

We (John and Ike) would like to also deeply thank co-author Mary Sitze for her work on this book. Mary took a later draft and dramatically added to the fictional family story line running through the book that powerfully brings the concepts and skills to life. She also spent many long hours revising, reorganizing, and honing the language of the text so that it now flows in an even more elegant, succinct, and graceful manner. Mary put her heart and soul into these pages, and it shows. We are so grateful for all the ways Mary contributed to this book.

We would like to thank Beth Barany and her team at Barany Consulting for shepherding us through the entire publication process. Her invaluable insight into many aspects of the book creation process, and her patience as the process took unexpected turns and far longer than we originally anticipated, are greatly appreciated.

We'd like to thank all those who have been part of our own growth, learning, and development. That includes the people in our trainings, particularly our immersion programs. Though they may be our students, we have learned as much from them as they learned from us. By attending our trainings, they have given us the opportunity and forum to continue learning. Thank you also to all our friends and colleagues in the community of NVC trainers and practitioners around the world and over the years who have been such a wonderful source of support, companionship, and inspiration.

I (John) feel a tremendous debt of gratitude to the many teachers who have shown the way and inspired me so profoundly. There have been so many, but the ones who have played a special role for me are: David Whyte, Eckhart Tolle, Deepak Chopra, Pema Chodron, and Wayne Dyer. And then there are the three, my holy trinity, who have been my greatest teachers, who have burned so brightly for me that they light up the sky: Marshall Rosenberg, Carl Rogers, and Mahatma Gandhi. A bow of honoring all the way down to the ground.

I (John) also want to thank my wife Schena for her steadfast love and support through all trials and tribulations. Thank you my love for always believing in me, and seeing what I cannot yet see. And thank you to my children for giving me an experience of love that is boundless and breathtaking. My family is the center of my world and the foundation from which I go out into the world to do my work, and then always return home. I have probably learned most of all from you.

I (Ike) would like to thank all the anonymous people who I've practiced my skills on, from people on 800 numbers and in other service capacities, to strangers on the street. And most of all, I want to thank my family, who have all suffered through my now almost twenty years of learning, much of it by trial and error, with emphasis on error.

I (Ike) would also like to acknowledge Claire Nuer and the Learning As Leadership (LearnAsLead.com) team. Though we do not reference their work directly, what I learned in their programs has strongly influenced my thinking in a number of ways that show up in this work. For example, the concept of first looking for my part in any situation came through Claire.

Of course, we owe a debt of gratitude to Marshall Rosenberg for his creation of Nonviolent Communication and the work of decades to spread it widely around the world. Our lives, and the lives of many others, have been indelibly bettered through this way of communicating. What we contribute stands upon the incredibly strong foundation that Marshall created.

Introduction
by Ike Lasater

Many years ago, I was walking with two female companions in downtown San Francisco when a man abruptly veered toward us and came right up into our faces. This man was about my height, but was about twenty years younger than I. He didn't touch anyone, but his posture and demeanor seemed to signal aggression.

I immediately went into fight mode. This guy was invading our space and was leaning in to me. His left hand was balled into a fist by his side. I felt very defensive, because I thought he was going to hit me. I presumed that the man might be drunk or high on something. He had debris in his hair as if he had slept outside the night before.

Seeing how much the man had frightened my companions, I felt certain I was justified in putting him on the ground and hurting him. In my jacked-up state, I remember thinking, "I've done all this Aikido practice. Now I'm going to take this guy down, and I'm going to take him down hard!"

I came within a flick of an eyelash of doing just that.

Then I had a glimmer of awareness. Before taking action, I said to the guy, "When you're this close I'm feeling afraid. Would you back up a couple of feet?"

The man's eyes widened a bit. He stood up straighter and stepped back.

I asked him what he wanted. "I want money," he said. He unclenched the fingers of his left hand to reveal the loose roll of quarters in his fist.

I felt a mixture of relief, annoyance, and confusion. I wasn't about to give this guy any money. I still felt closed—still in fight mode—on account of the way he had appeared to threaten me and my friends.

Somehow, recognizing how closed off I was feeling had allowed me to be curious. I asked the man, "Do you want this money because you want some support?"

His face softened, and he knocked off this spontaneous lyric:

"Yeah, man.
I want support, I want care,
I want tenderness, I want love."

I heard myself exhale and felt my heart open. Reaching into my pocket, I drew out a bill, folded it up, and extended it to the man. He glanced down at the offering, and back up at me. Then he pressed his head against my chest, and started to cry. "Thank you," he said, before stumbling off.

I stood there, stunned at all that had just gone down. The man and I had said so little to each other. So what had changed him? What had changed me? How did two strangers shift so rapidly away from violence and into a state of connection?

I cringe to think about what could have happened if I had gone with my initial reaction. Suppose I had gotten violent with this guy? Imagine how much damage he and I could have done to each other, and how the gulf between us could have grown.

Somehow, I'd been able to summon the awareness that *I didn't have to give in to my adrenaline-fueled fight response.* For a crucial fraction of a second, I had recognized the fact that I could make another choice. That awareness had made all the difference in the outcome of our meeting on the street.

I've returned to the memory of that encounter many times. For me, it is a reminder that we can respond to any challenge in our lives from a space of clear-headedness and compassion. With sufficient awareness, we can skip the panicked "fight-flight-or-freeze" instinct in favor of a response that leaves far less damage in its wake. In this way, we can have the sorts of meaningful interactions that we all want and so rarely get.

Few of us will regularly find ourselves face-to-face with a threatening stranger—at least I hope so. Yet all of us daily experience some version of a stress-based reaction, usually many times each day. And all of us have to deal with the fallout from our knee-jerk reactions.

Maybe you find yourself set off by how your child speaks to you (or doesn't) in the mornings. Maybe you are driven to distraction by the questions your mother asks you on the phone. Maybe you find yourself silently fuming over the way a co-worker tosses another file on your desk.

Your reaction to these personal "triggers" might be to yell or to withdraw. You may unconsciously seek ways to punish the other person. You may endlessly replay the injustice in your mind and complain about it to someone else. Or you may find the tension you're feeling is so uncomfortable that you try to blot it out through some means of escape.

In short, you may react instead of really choosing how you want to respond. You may adopt any number of socially sanctioned and ostensibly logical tactics, but at the cost of your own and others' greater peace.

Think of this book in your hands as a much-needed "operating manual" for our common relationship with conflict. If there's anything difficult, scary, or unpleasant that you grapple with in your life—and we all do!—then let this book be your ticket to greater clarity and fewer regrets. Learn how to respond with heart and eyes wide open to the friction and setbacks you meet with each day. Experiment with the awareness techniques that can help you listen and communicate in a way that helps you make better decisions—and build stronger relationships—in everything that you do.

This book is a distillation of over ten years of teaching and learning with my Mediate Your Life training partner, John Kinyon. It's because these insights have made such a difference in our own lives that we are compelled to share them with you. We can't predict exactly what you'll do with the life-changing information in this book, but we can promise that you will never regret "Choosing Peace."

Thanks for joining us on the journey.

Ike Lasater
New Haven, Connecticut
May 2014

1 | Choosing Peace
Creating Connection to Reduce Conflict

"In all situations, it is my response that decides whether a crisis will be escalated or de-escalated, and a person humanized or de-humanized."
—*Johann Wolfgang von Goethe*

Sally hadn't known it was possible to slam a door so hard. She half-ran, half-stumbled down the driveway, her eyes blurred with angry tears. This was supposed to be the start of a special week. It had been almost five years since she and her siblings had been together in the same place. Sally was determined to make it a great visit for all of them—and especially for Mom, who would soon be released from the hospital.

Gerry had made the overseas flight because Sally had begged him to come see why their mother could no longer live alone. Peg might not be willing to admit it yet, but she didn't stop by Mom's place everyday like Sally did. Sally had been counting on Gerry to back her up on the difficult decisions to be made about their mother's care. Instead, the siblings' first meeting at their mother's house felt tense. In short order, all three had said things they would later regret, and the conversation had devolved into shouting and accusations. That's when Sally had fled the scene and slammed the door.

Normally, Sally might have called her husband, but she had quarreled with him that very morning about which of them was going to take off work for an emergency parent-teacher conference. Sally dialed her friend Alicia instead. "Why is this happening to my family?" Sally wept. "We're falling apart."

* * * * * *

Conflicts are a fact of life. Everywhere that there are human relationships, there will also be conflicts. Rare is the person who relishes being in the midst of conflict. Many people prefer to avoid conflicts, or to pretend that conflicts don't exist. Some even try to avoid the word "conflict," instead substituting words such as "friction" or "disagreement." However you name it, the experience of challenge, difficulty, and stress is universal and nearly omnipresent in our lives.

Broadly defined, conflict is any sort of tension, opposition, or difference that creates feelings of pain and separation. In the traditional sense, conflict exists any time two or more individuals are in dispute. Most days, you will find yourself a witness to this kind of conflict. Maybe you see a fellow commuter argue with the bus driver, or you observe two children fighting over a toy. Most days, you will also find yourself directly embroiled in one or more conflicts. Perhaps you find yourself at odds with a co-worker, or you clash with a family member over scheduling or household chores.

Conflicts also occur between different aspects of your own mind, as happens when you are torn over a difficult decision. A huge factor in how you respond to external conflicts is how you deal with what happens to you internally. As a human being, you will inevitably experience a physiological response to anything that you perceive as a conflict. In that moment of reaction, your thinking may literally become impaired—so much so, that it can be difficult to choose a response that you will feel good about later.

Sally found herself in conflict with her siblings, but also with herself. Like her brother and sister, she found herself saying hurtful things that she now wished she could take back. She ended up slamming the door and cutting off communication rather than continuing a conversation that was making her upset. Was there anything Sally could have done to make the sibling meeting go more smoothly? And how could she repair the damage caused by their communication breakdown?

A NEW APPROACH TO CONFLICT AND MEDIATION

The Mediate Your Life program begins with three premises:

1. Conflict is inherent in all relationships, including the one you have with yourself.
2. We are all of us vulnerable to the brain's "fight-flight-freeze" survival response, a now mostly unhelpful pattern of reaction in our modern world (we will refer to this response interchangeably as fight or flight, fight-flight-freeze, or stress response).
3. Through our choice of language and awareness, we can overcome the fight or flight pattern and turn our daily conflicts into opportunities for connection.

Let's explore what follows from each of those three premises.

Conflict is inevitable. Sometimes just the simple decision to accept this fact can help us become more comfortable in the face of conflict.

Conflicts are bound to happen because we are pattern-recognition creatures. If you've ever found yourself rehashing the same old ground with a partner, you know something about patterns and how difficult it can be to break out of them.

Each of us has tender spots or "trigger points" that developed as a result of our individual histories and these can activate a fight-flight-freeze reaction.

Conflicts happen because we humans are together, but separate. The clearer we are on this point, the more likely we'll remember how to make the connections we want.

Because we can't ever truly get inside someone else's experience, it's all too easy to misunderstand each other. How often do we misinterpret or over-interpret another person's actions as hostile to our own interests? How often do we miss someone else's signal because it was unintelligible to us? Until we have the ability to "mind-meld," opportunities for miscommunication and conflict will abound.

For now, the mind-meld is the stuff of science fiction. The "lizard brain" is not. Brain science has shown us how parts of the human brain may conspire against us in conflict situations. The amygdala (sometimes jokingly referred to as the "lizard brain") is where our fight-flight-freeze and emotional responses originate. Its role is quite different from that of the neo-cortex, which is responsible for self-direction or "executive functioning." The neural pathways between these two parts of the brain are relatively weak, which means that our most base emotions (fear, fury) can easily get the best of us.

The weak connection between lizard brain and neo-cortex is good news if you're being chased by a bear. In that context, you definitely want your body putting all its energies into moving your legs as quickly as possible without any conscious thought. But it's not great news when a family member makes an off-hand comment that triggers you into a high-adrenaline state.

If you've never practiced how to respond to conflict, a triggering comment can take you places you didn't intend to go. If your stress response tends toward **fight**, you may say or shout something that is more cutting than it is helpful. You may physically express yourself in a way that is intimidating or dangerous to those around you.

If your fight-flight-freeze response tends toward **flight or freeze**, you may run away to avoid the confrontation, or else find yourself tongue-tied and stuck in place.

Some people find themselves experiencing multiple stress responses, as Sally did when she first fought with her siblings and then felt compelled to escape.

Could it ever be otherwise? Reacting in these ways to conflict situations wastes so much energy. How wonderful it would be if we could live our lives without the constant tumult—without bouncing off each other and reacting to stimuli like the little metal balls in a pinball machine.

The Mediate Your Life approach offers an entirely different way of being in conflict. Its focus is on *responding* to conflict rather than just reacting to it.

Our approach is not invested in figuring out who's right or wrong in the midst of conflict, whose strategy is best, or what you have to do to "win." When you "mediate your life," you cultivate an entirely new set of go-to habits for the moments when you are confronted with a difficult situation. With practice, you can grow accustomed to adopting a bird's-eye view of the conflict and can select your words and body language to ensure that everyone involved in the conflict has the opportunity to try to hear each other fully.

"To hear each other fully" isn't as simple as it may sound. In fact, it can be one of the hardest things you ever learn to do. There's nothing touchy-feely about that skill. For most people, developing the ability to respond to others with compassionate, open ears requires a lot of practice and "re-wiring" of old conflict habits.

When you can manage the discomfort of conflict and stay focused in your disagreements long enough to hear not only the words, but also the motivations behind the words, something incredible happens. When you can "mediate" your internal reactions by sorting them out in tandem with the needs of everyone else present, you may find that the outcome exceeds your wildest expectations.

* * * * *

Sally hadn't expected that sorting out Mom's crisis was going to be easy. But she had assumed that her brother and sister would listen to her and would do what they could to help. Instead, it seemed to Sally that both siblings had been skeptical and resistant. Peg thought it was "rude and disrespectful" to try to coax their mother to do anything she didn't want to do. Gerry expressed doubt that their mother's living situation was as dire as Sally had made it out to be. He grew defensive and angry when Sally told him that he lived too far away and so he couldn't possibly know what was going on.

Sally gripped the steering wheel more tightly as she remembered the words that she and Gerry had spoken to each other next.

"Don't you think you're overstepping here?" Gerry had asked Sally. "Just because you never moved away doesn't mean that you're in charge. Mom's still Mom. And she has other children besides just you."

Sally had felt her cheeks grow hot with fury and humiliation. "Mom's not still Mom. If you cared enough to come home more often, you would know that. And I might as well be Mom's only child, because I'm the only one who gives a damn about her well-being!"

Sally had seen the flashes of anguish and outrage on her siblings' faces. Overwhelmed by her own feelings of hurt and frustration and scared that she was about to break down, she had no idea what she could do next. That's when her instinct for self-protection took over and she ran away.

WHAT DOES IT MEAN TO "MEDIATE YOUR LIFE?"

The word "mediate" comes from a Latin root that means "in the middle" or "in-between." To mediate is to facilitate communication between two or more individuals or groups.

Whether or not you're a professional mediator, the odds are good that you do some mediating every day. Sometimes it may be over a dispute that is external to you, as happens when two children both want the same toy and you help them to work out a solution. Or maybe you've played informal mediator between yourself and another person, when you tried to listen deeply to the neighbor with whom you're always butting heads. Perhaps you often find yourself mediating an internal struggle between different parts of yourself, as happens when a part of you clings to the security of a boring, but stable job, while another part of you craves a more interesting, but less secure type of work.

Mediation from our approach tries to bring about empathic understanding and connection between opposing sides. Note that getting two individuals to understand each other's perspectives is not the same as getting them to agree. In a successful mediation, the people who were formerly estranged end up feeling connected to each other because they recognize their mutually held human motivations. Skillful mediation uses connection to guide everyone toward a formal resolution to the dispute.

Implicitly, we're always *trying* to mediate the conflicts we encounter in various contexts. However, relatively few people are able to mediate effectively. That's because certain essential skills are very rarely taught—even in formal mediator trainings.

The Mediate Your Life trainings and practice sessions are designed to give you those crucial skills while also sharpening your awareness of different types of conflict situations. By showing you how to more consistently access the most calm, clear-eyed and empathetic version of yourself, they allow you to use and strengthen the mediator instincts you may already possess.

The Mediate Your Life approach can also help you to cut through the conflicts within yourself. It helps you to navigate the big questions, including:

- How do I build a satisfying life?
- How can I figure out "what is" right now?
- How do I create meaning in all I do?
- How do I get clear about what I want to create in my life?
- How do I live my life in a way that is true to myself, and not to others' expectations?
- How can I figure out who and what is most important to me?
- How will I spend my time?
- How do I find the courage to express myself authentically?
- How can I interact with others so all of us are more likely to get what we want and need?
- How do I put any of the above into action once I know it? (And how do I keep knowing it?)

This is serious stuff! It's nothing less than choosing how you want to live and act in every part of your life. It's figuring out how to *be*, moment to moment, such that you can act in accordance with your deepest values.

RESPONDING, NOT REACTING

By the time you finish reading this book, we hope you'll feel excited enough to embrace an entirely new way to be in conflict. Remember, conflicts are a fact of life. The radical idea at the core of the Mediate Your Life program is that you can actually get comfortable with conflict. When you learn to "mediate" your internal reactions along with other people's needs, amazing things will happen. That's because you will be *responding* to conflict, rather than just *reacting* to it. Yes, you've heard us say that before. But now, let's unpack that idea.

To explain the difference between "responding" and "reacting," it's worth returning to the quotation that opened this chapter—a quote that is widely attributed to the 19th century German philosopher, Johann Wolfgang von Goethe.

"In all situations,
it is my response that decides
whether a crisis will be escalated or de-escalated,
and a person humanized or de-humanized."

Let's examine that quote more closely, line by line, and let's consider it through the lens of some hypothetical examples.

"In ALL situations..."
At every moment of our lives, we must choose what to do next.

> Example A: When you're running late and someone cuts you off in traffic.
> Example B: When someone else's success causes you to doubt yourself.
> Example C: When a family member's words remind you of a past hurt.

Each of these examples represents a situation or a sudden rush of feeling, that can knock you off balance. What happens next?

"... it is my response that decides..."

If you can stop yourself from reacting out of the irritation or pain caused by a stressful situation, then you can have a lot of power over what happens next. That's because your response will determine...

"... if a crisis is escalated or de-escalated ..."

The "crisis" here can refer to any sort of difficulty or tension. Your response will have clear consequences. Things are going to get easier or more complicated as a result.

"... and a person humanized or de-humanized."

If you can respond (out of choice), rather than react (out of the fight or flight pattern), whatever you do next will rely heavily on your *perception* of the person or persons involved.

To "de-humanize" someone may sound extreme. But think about the last time you were in the midst of an adrenaline-spiking disagreement with someone else. Or think about the last time somebody did or said something to you that left you feeling crushed. Wasn't it quite easy, in that moment, to peg the other person as the embodiment of everything you hated and feared?

And isn't that reaction kind of normal? Well, yes.

What isn't "normal," or at least not normally modeled for us, is how to humanize, or empathize, with someone else in the midst of a frustrating exchange. We're more likely to want to thump the other person on the head than to try to imagine him or her as a fellow human with needs much like our own.

This is why we began the Mediate Your Life program: to share a nearly foolproof formula for how you can respond, rather than react, to difficult situations. Once you become aware of your brain's particular fight-flight-freeze pattern, you can learn how to overcome it. Then you are free to respond in a way that can turn your daily conflicts into opportunities for connection.

Let's run through our hypothetical examples to see what that would look like.

Example A:
When you're running late and someone cuts you off in traffic.

When that jackass cuts you off in traffic on a day that you're already running late, you slam on the horn and signal your irritation with your middle finger.

—OR—

You breathe deeply in response to the feeling of clench in your gut. After taking a moment to work through your exasperation, you try to imagine what might be going on for the distracted driver in that other car. Feeling a flicker of empathy for the other driver, you start to feel calmer about how to handle your own time-crunch.

The second response might feel a whole lot less satisfying in the heat of the moment. But ask yourself: In which scenario did you de-escalate the crisis? In which were you and all the other people around you safer? And in which did you enjoy more control?

Example B:
When someone else's success causes you to doubt yourself.

When your co-worker is singled out for praise at a public work function, you feel happiness for your co-worker (whom you admire) along with a flood of self-doubt; you mentally berate yourself for not being good enough or worthy enough to rise to the top.

—OR—

You notice your feelings of agitation and sadness and realize how much you value knowing that you are contributing at work. From this realization flows another: how important it is to you to care about the people you work with and to celebrate their successes. So you focus on feeling and expressing gratitude for your co-worker. Later, you reflect on how some of your own contributions have been positively received by your workmates and also how you might seek constructive feedback to continue to improve your at-work performance.

Again, the second scenario is the more challenging one. True, there was no resentment toward the co-worker, but there was a reflexive self-criticism, and this de-humanized you! We de-humanize ourselves—and limit what we can contribute to the world—each time we slip into the all-too-easy spiral of shame and self-recrimination.

Example C:
When a family member's words remind you of a past hurt.

When you confide to your cousin that you've decided to become a teacher, she expresses surprise, because, in her words, "You weren't exactly an A-student." You cover up your anger and embarrassment by blurting: "Why do you always try to make me feel lousy about myself?"

—OR—

After taking the necessary steps to take in your cousin's observation without having a bad reaction to it, you offer an honest reply: "It's true I didn't have a perfect grade point average. But remember how supportive my teachers were the year my folks got divorced and I was in a really bad space? And remember how Mr. Vigiano convinced me to try out for the debate team? I want to help other kids the way my teachers helped me."

The second scenario allows for the possibility that your cousin hadn't intended for her words to register a criticism. It also recognizes that she might be feeling uncomfortable at the prospect of you changing your accustomed role in the family. You don't have to ignore the fact that your cousin's surprise and her particular choice of words "hit you in the gut," but you can take steps that allow you to move through the hurt as you try to figure out where your cousin was coming from. The words you wanted to hurl back at her ("Why do you *always*...?") hint that you and she may both be feeling constrained by your childhood identities and/or that you carry judgments about each other that are getting in the way of clear communication. To help your cousin understand your career shift, you can choose to share more of your reasons for wanting to be a teacher, even if some of them leave you feeling vulnerable. The conversation that follows will be all the smoother if you and your cousin can approach each other from a space of trust and assumed goodwill. Even if it's only you who intentionally occupies this space, your interactions with your cousin will likely be marked by greater kindness and honesty.

Whew! Each of the alternate scenarios above shows all that becomes possible when you mediate your internal reactions and choose to be curious about the other person's perspective, such that you can try and "get" where she is coming from. When you respond rather than react to others' words and actions, your response really will decide "if a crisis is escalated or de-escalated and if the people around you are humanized or de-humanized." As you probably noticed, it's the de-humanizing of others (and of ourselves) that often leads us into trouble.

OUR ROOTS IN NONVIOLENT COMMUNICATION (NVC)

The Mediate Your Life approach is steeped in the language of Nonviolent Communication (NVC), a linguistic model created by the world-famous clinical psychologist, Marshall

Rosenberg. Dr. Rosenberg created NVC in the 1960s to reduce violence and spread peace-building skills around the world. In the decades since, he has offered NVC trainings and conflict resolution sessions in over 60 countries, sometimes stepping in to facilitate conflicts in war-torn regions of the globe.

Nonviolent Communication provides a structure, or "how-to," that aligns with many of humanity's spiritual traditions. It gives us a way to focus our mental attention on "what is," stripped of all our prior assumptions and prejudices. In this way, NVC allows us to view the world with fresh eyes and hearts, so we can more often choose to respond with compassion.

We encountered NVC's transformative worldview in the 1990s, and were so taken with it that we immediately began to integrate it into our lives and soon began teaching it to others. We quickly found, however, that the basic NVC model was not sufficient in stressful situations, when the fight or flight reaction was triggered. In the moments we most needed NVC, it was often difficult to access. In the moments when we were especially defensive or inflamed, NVC could feel like a very elusive tool, indeed.

We noticed a similar pattern in our trainings, in which we sought to teach people to mediate conflicts with NVC. We had assumed mediation simply consisted of a mediator supporting two or more people to resolve their conflicts. We found this to be quite a challenge. In order for mediators to be maximally effective, they needed to be able to mediate their own internal conflicts, especially those that arose in reaction to their clients. They also needed more of a structure to handle the different types of disputes and communication pitfalls that their clients brought their way. In these contexts, NVC on its own terms was not enough.

As a result of this discovery, we began to create our own step-by-step guides, or "maps," to navigate the territory of different types of conflict situations. We devised a specific map for each situation and incorporated them into our trainings.

Over time, we developed nuanced exercises to let our participants practice how to navigate internal and interpersonal conflicts with the help of what we initially referred to as our "NVC Mediation" method.

Eventually, NVC Mediation became Mediate Your Life, especially once we took on the mission of supporting individuals to mediate their lives and their internal conflicts by developing a keen awareness of their fight or flight patterns. So, while our work started with formal mediation (between two other people), it expanded to include all forms of conflict a person can experience: within oneself, between oneself and others, and between others.

Nonetheless, Nonviolent Communication remains a crucial part of Mediate Your Life's DNA, not least because we (John and Ike) came together as training partners thanks to our shared respect for NVC and an experience made possible by Marshall Rosenberg.

In late 2001, Dr. Rosenberg had been planning a trip to Pakistan to offer NVC trainings to Afghan refugees. Independently of each other, we both had asked permission to tag along. Dr. Rosenberg graciously said yes. Remember, this was in the wake of 9/11 and the dawn of the U.S. war in Afghanistan, so that region of the world was growing increasingly unpredictable. Dr. Rosenberg eventually decided not to travel to Pakistan, due to very real concerns about safety. We were already there, and we ended up offering three days of training to Afghan elders in Peshawar, which is 50 kilometers (31 miles) from the Pakistan-Afghan border.

It was astonishing to witness how effectively NVC bridged immense cultural and linguistic divides. We felt a deep connection with the elders as we witnessed how powerful it was for them to be heard about what was important to them. Then, on the final day of training, the elders fell out over whether we should be allowed to visit the mosque during prayers. With the help of our translator, we used NVC mediation to sort out everyone's views on the question and eventually came to an agreement that worked for all. One of the elders came up to us afterward with tears in his eyes and said the words we will never forget: "*If we could do this* [sort out crises with NVC mediation], *we would have no need for war.*"

Galvanized by that experience, we began offering regular NVC mediation trainings in the San Francisco Bay area, where we both then lived with our respective families. We started with eight-week classes and some weekend workshops. For the next 11 years, in some guise or another, we kept building on what would become the Mediate Your Life approach and devising the practice exercises that would best allow our students to develop entirely new habits in the midst of conflicts.

Both of us had our unique strengths as trainers, but we found a particular synergy when we lead trainings together. Eventually, we co-designed our "dream training" and turned it into a reality. That first year of the NVC Mediation "Immersion Program" was a bit rocky. Thanks to the generous feedback from our earliest students, we kept refining the immersion experience until students could absorb the material at an accelerated rate while also remaining in total control of their learning. From the beginning, we urged students to use *real* conflicts from their lives in the training exercises, including any conflict that might arise between students or even between a student and one of us. The authenticity of the exercises demonstrates how reliable the Mediate Your Life maps can be. They also offer the students some instant results. We've never regretted the "real conflicts" model, as it gives our students the confidence to apply the Mediate Your Life approach to any challenge in their lives and communities.

Over the past decade, we have led immersion programs in Australia, Poland, and Korea, as well as in multiple locations across the United States. (See Appendix G for more about our trainings.) Through the years, we have grown along with our students, some of whom now co-facilitate our trainings and have launched Mediate Your Life-based consultancies of their own. We could never have foreseen how a partnership born out of our mutual enthusiasm for NVC would gradually evolve into a globally recognized method for managing conflict in every possible context, and for "choosing peace" in the before, during and after of conflict resolution. We've dedicated our professional lives to this work because it works. We're also hooked because we've seen how the Mediate Your Life approach has transformed our own lives.

WHY THIS WORK IS IMPORTANT TO IKE

Out of everything I've tried, from Iyengar Yoga to Soto Zen, from voice dialogue and psychotherapy to Aikido, nothing has been as effective as the approach I use now.

For the positive transformation of my personal life, I have relied on Nonviolent Communication and the Mediate Your Life approach that John Kinyon and I developed out of our shared roots in NVC. I use the skills I teach every day. They help me to align my actions with my values. As I shared in the introduction to this book, if I value treating people with respect, then I'm not being consistent with that value when I contemplate punching a man on the street. Most of the spiritual and therapeutic approaches I've studied lay out the ideals to follow, but they don't provide me with the tools to let me assess *in real time* whether or not my behavior is aligned with those ideals.

The Mediate Your Life approach is the most effective path I've found to help me wake up and to stay awake. It helps me to be aware of when I'm doing or saying things that I'm likely to regret, and it give me the means to make a course correction. This allows me to re-establish who I am and who I want to be as expressed by my conduct. I believe I create myself by my conduct, and that's a tenet of the Mediate Your Life approach. Heartfelt principles and values are fine and good. But, if we can't manifest them in all we do and say, then they become occasions for self-criticism and self-punishment.

With the Mediate Your Life approach, you become aware of your conduct, and can reflect on how it is and is not consistent with your values, while skipping the de-energizing trap of self-blame. Believe me when I say that this is not about denial or "letting yourself off easy." It's a strategy for self-improvement. Because beating yourself up or trying to use shame to motivate yourself into doing something (or *not* doing something) often has the paradoxical effect of reinforcing the behavior that you are distressed about.

The path I'm on with Mediate Your Life has given me tools to engage with people who have vastly different life experiences than my own. By listening to others in the ways that NVC and Mediate Your Life make possible, I've gotten as close as I've ever been to "walking in another person's shoes," and comprehending what motivates and animates that person in a particular situation. Having tapped that understanding, I feel care toward people I don't know well—and that has been both very humbling and very satisfying to me.

For me, the work of sharing the Mediate Your Life approach is urgent: I'm in my sixties and have children and grandchildren. I care deeply about the world that we're leaving for them and for all children. That's why I want the Mediate Your Life program to help you and those you love to live more fulfilling and satisfying lives. If it helps one person, that is a good unto itself. But by altering how each of us respond to even the smallest conflicts, we can—person by person, community by community—build the habits of empathy and collaboration that just may bridge the giant chasms that divide us. The habits laid out in the Mediate Your Life program can change a life. They also may be literally life-saving, as we respond to climate change, religious conflicts, wars over resources, and all the other challenges that threaten us as a species.

WHY THIS WORK IS IMPORTANT TO JOHN

I believe that a person can resolve and heal from any conflict. I believe that truly anyone can learn to do this, so long as he or she is willing to put in the time. And I believe that the insights of the Mediate Your Life program will contribute to the positive evolution of humanity. Just as passing on the light of a single candle can eventually illuminate a room to brilliance, so too can a single student of the Mediate Your Life approach eventually help to transform how our human species responds to conflict.

Without NVC and the work of Mediate Your Life, I would be living a very different life. Today I am fortunate to be very happily married, with three happy, healthy, thriving children. Believe me, none of this would have been possible were it not for NVC mediation. I don't believe I would be married today, and I certainly wouldn't know what to do as a parent, without the guidance of the very skills that I'm proud to teach.

Our Mediate Your Life approach uses a "three-chair model" as its basic framework. Transformation happens by exposing two opposing perspectives to an empathetic third presence. To me this triad represents a holy trinity of sorts, a sacred geometry in which opposing forces find synthesis and integration at a higher order of functioning. Using this approach takes some care, but it's well worth it. Ultimately, it harnesses the tremendous energy and power that is latent in all conflict and directs that energy into more positive directions.

Both Ike and I feel an enormous gratitude to Marshall Rosenberg for the legacy he has passed on to us and to many, many others around the world. We'll continue to honor that legacy through our Mediate Your Life work, because we can't imagine not sharing the skills that we know, first-hand, can repair even the most broken and seemingly hopeless relationships.

This ability to create connection from conflict is now an imperative. The sustainability of our daily lives—and of the planet—depends upon it.

The Goals Of This Book

Think for a moment about your own experience and the patterns you notice in your life:

- Do you tend to avoid conflict and the people you have disagreements with?
- Do you find yourself feeling rattled long after a stressful event? Do you endlessly replay the event in your mind and re-live the unpleasant feelings that came with it?
- Do you beat yourself up over things you did or said—or things you failed to do and say? Do you have the voice of the relentless self-critic in your head?
- When you get angry with someone, do you see him or her as "the bad guy?"
- When someone makes suggestions for things you could do differently, do you find yourself becoming defensive and angry?
- Do you sometimes respond to conflict situations by giving someone the "cold shoulder"; i.e., by pointedly pretending that the other person doesn't exist?

If you answered "yes" to any of the above, then this book is for you.

If you would like to have more satisfying and engaging relationships, this book is for you.

If you would like to get absolutely clear about who you are, who you still want to be, and the next steps to living your best possible life, then this book is definitely for you.

Think of this book as your guide to some of the trickiest, stickiest moments of your life.

Let what you read in these pages be the equivalent of a clear-headed friend at your elbow, the one who helps you remember to breathe and remain calm whenever you are in a situation like Sally's. With enough practice, ultimately *you* will be that clear-headed friend. You will build a better life—for yourself and others—by changing how you respond to conflicts.

What are the recurring conflicts in your life right now? Maybe there is a lot of distrust in your personal relationships or maybe the fight or flight reaction kicks in easily for you and for the people closest to you. Maybe you have habitual ways of responding to conflict that you know are the equivalent of pouring gasoline on a fire, exacerbating the crisis instead of diminishing it.

Which would you rather do? Develop the capacity to catch yourself and choose the words that will make a situation better? Or continue the habits and patterns that intensify the conflicts in your personal life and in the wider world?

This book, and the whole of the Mediate Your Life book series, will help you to choose. If you study the Mediate Your Life approach and consistently practice it, we predict that you will:

- Recognize your fight-flight-freeze stress patterns and be able to shift out of them
- More often respond to conflicts in ways that you feel good about later
- Find a softer way to approach difficult situations
- Be able to listen more skillfully, and without judging another person's perspective as "wrong" or "bad"
- Learn to be clearer in your own communications and to help others be clearer
- Be kinder to yourself and to those close to you
- Have a quality of interaction with others that is deeper
- Create more peace and compassion in your life

HOW TO USE THIS BOOK

In the past decade, the Mediate Your Life workshops and immersion programs have attracted thousands of students from all over the world. Many have urged us to publish our training manual and to write books about our NVC mediation approach so our work could reach an even wider audience. A lot of our students go on to teach the Mediate Your Life approach to others in their communities and workplaces, and they, too, have asked for a resource like the one you hold in your hands.

We're thrilled to share the awareness techniques and practice exercises that we have developed in our Mediate Your Life immersion programs. However, as our students can tell you, this material is not something you can read once and then expect instant results. Seeing real change will require some more effort. To benefit from the tools inside this book, you'll need to try them out for yourself through experiment and play. This book will support you in shedding less productive ways of interacting and replacing them with more effective communication patterns and reflexes.

Just as you can't read a book about swimming and suddenly know how to swim, you also can't read a book about communicating in a different way and be able to do it perfectly on your very first try. Consider this book a first step in the process of acquiring a whole new mindset. To extend the swimming metaphor, you will first dip your toe in the water and then get your feet wet. Eventually, you'll work up to where you are comfortable in the shallows, and then you'll go deeper and deeper until you are able to swim from one beach to the next.

If you're brand new to NVC mediation, then this book will help you get your feet wet. If you already have some experience, it will deepen your understanding of the basics and increase your confidence. If you've been working with NVC mediation for a long time, then you may enjoy this book for how it enhances your capacity to embody and teach the skills that you use every day.

Wherever you are in your process, we invite you to take what you need from this book and to allow the parts that make the most sense to you to seep into your interactions. Each story in this book serves as a life buoy and lighthouse. Let them prop you up whenever you need a little help and let them guide you to safety.

Unlike other programs for self-improvement, you don't need to invest in a lot of special equipment or set aside enormous blocks of time to make progress toward your goals. All we ask is that you take personally everything that you read in these pages. That is, take it in and make it your own. As you read, do your best to try and live this book, so you can begin to see for yourself all there is to gain from its approach. Stick with it, and you'll get a glimpse of what your life can be like when you are more often at peace with yourself and are able to connect—really connect—with others. Work through the practice suggestions, and you will notice in yourself a decreased level of anxiety and a far greater capacity to handle difficult conversations.

Use the practice exercises to reflect on whatever happens in your daily life so you can learn from it. All of it. There is no failure here, only more fodder for growth. Use each "Practice Pause" when it shows up in the text. If you really want to turbo-charge your learning, find a practice partner so together you can go through the seventeen techniques we share. If you can't find a local partner, then find one in the Mediate Your Life network via our book page at http://www.mediate yourlife.com/choosingpeace.

Notice opportunities to practice as you move through your day. What's terrific about these skills is that you can practice them literally anywhere, at any moment, and with anyone with whom you have interactions. This includes everyone—from your buddies to your boss to the barista in your neighborhood coffee shop. So don't let any excuse get in the way of your commitment to use this book. The sooner you start, the sooner you can begin creating more meaningful relationships and building the life you want. And the sooner the people who share your life will begin to notice the change in you.

HOW THIS BOOK IS ORGANIZED

This, the first volume in the Mediate Your Life series, covers the most foundational content of our method. Later books will walk you through the "maps" in our mediation model. Most of the chapters in this book present the building blocks of NVC as we teach them in our programs. If the entire Mediate Your Life series is an operating manual on how to fly an airplane, then this volume is the essential overview of how to read the dials in the cockpit.

Even if you never read any of the other volumes in the Mediate Your Life series, as long as you move diligently through the practice exercises in this first book, you will still feel a greater sense of peace and control over your reactions.

Chapters 2-6 offer a crystal clear overview of the NVC model as it is taught in our Mediate Your Life programs. NVC, or Nonviolent Communication, sometimes goes by other names, including Compassionate Communication or Collaborative Communication. However it is labeled, the NVC model is built upon four components of communication: Observations, Feelings, Needs, and Requests. Sometimes these four components are referred to by the acronym OFNR. When you have enough experience with it, OFNR can profoundly alter how you perceive the world and your negotiations within it.

Chapter 2 lays the groundwork for understanding how to use the four components of communication. It describes the psychological benefits of being heard and how you can use OFNR plus empathetic listening to produce the all-important "shift," or temporary lifting of tensions, between people who are at odds with each other.

Chapter 3 draws the distinction between observations and judgments. You may think you know the difference already, but this chapter shows how frequently most of us mix them up, particularly in conflict situations.

Chapter 4 is all about feelings and the perils of trying to access and interpret them when emotions are running high. The way we talk about our feelings can fuel a conflict or can help resolve it. This chapter shows how to talk about feelings in a way that makes the speaker's intentions clearer and reduces agitation in both the listener and the speaker.

Chapter 5 distinguishes between a need and a strategy. After taking care to define a "need" in NVC terms, it shows why finding out what a person needs can be a remarkably clarifying and calming piece of information, particularly in moments of conflict. Chapter 5 also makes plain the difference between needs and strategies and how to find the need when you are only aware of your strategy.

Chapter 6 delivers a simple but astonishing message about making requests. If you're someone who struggles to know what you want, or what the people around you want, then this chapter may blow your mind. After differentiating between requests and demands, it explains how to make requests that are maximally effective.

The **Conclusion** brings back the intention of this book: to support you in learning the skills to create space between a stimulus and your fight or flight response so that you have the chance to choose peace. If you see the possibilities for improving your connection to yourself and others in the pages of this book, then you will also be interested in the glimpse we give of the territory we will cover in the rest of the Mediate Your Life series.

The **Epilogue** by John Kinyon is not so much an ending as it is a gateway to new possibilities. This final chapter offers a preview of a new way to be as John reflects on the legacy of

Marshall Rosenberg. Through stories of Marshall's example, John highlights the importance of going beyond language to embody the awareness that the distinctions and skills in this book point to. This awareness is the key to choosing peace.

* * * * * *

Sally had pulled her car over to the side of the road so she could continue her call with Alicia. She could feel the tension in her body start to dissipate as she spoke with her longtime friend.

"It sounds like you're feeling scared and overwhelmed right now," Alicia was saying. "I wonder if you might need some support and rest."

"Yes!" Sally was surprised when the word came out as a sob. It just felt so good to hear someone put words to all the anger and confusion she had just been experiencing.

"I'm guessing that your siblings might be feeling scared and sad about how things are going," Alicia continued. "I wonder if they need to hear that they matter, and that they contribute in some way to your mother and to you."

"Well, they do contribute," Sally replied. "Peg always comes around on the rare weekends that she doesn't have to work. And even Gerry does a good job of keeping Mom's spirits up. She loves the silly little postcards he sends her. But now I really need Gerry and Peg to get serious…"

"Can you tell me what you mean by 'serious?' Do you have a specific request for either of them?"

Ten minutes later, Sally was back at her mother's house, feeling a mixture of relief and trepidation at the sight of her sister's car in the driveway. She took a deep breath as she mentally rehearsed the apology and requests that she had practiced saying out loud to Alicia. Sally knew this wouldn't be easy, but she loved her siblings and was determined that a stress reaction would NOT get the better of her again. Having recognized which of Gerry's words had made her so angry would help. Remembering OFNR would help, too. Feeling hopeful and calm, Sally strode up the walkway of her childhood home and knocked lightly on the door before letting herself inside.

2 Clarity in Communication
Escaping the Trap
of Our Own Interpretations

*"Between stimulus and response there is a space.
In that space is our power to choose our response.
In our response lies our growth and our freedom."
—Man's Search for Meaning
by Victor E. Frankl*

Peg sat with one knee twisted awkwardly beneath her on the sofa. With her head tipped back just so, she could see the furry layer of dust that had accumulated on the blades of Mom's ceiling fan. She thought about dragging out the stepladder so she could clean it off, but Gerry was pacing too much for that.

"Since when did Sally become such the expert, I'd like to know!" Gerry raked his fingers through his hair until half of it stood on end. He stalked the carpet, stabbing the air with one agitated finger as he spoke. "Did you hear her call us worthless? And where does she get off saying those things to us about Mom?"

"Sally's being totally selfish," Peg sighed. Her sister's words had stung. So much so, that Peg had wanted to cry. She hadn't let herself, because she didn't want Sally to know that anything she did affected her.

Gerry grabbed for his cell phone so he could dial up their sister and continue the fight. "Sally says Mom has memory problems?" Gerry let out a hoarse laugh. "I'd say the person having memory problems is the little sister who studied freaking 'medical anthropology' in college and now thinks she's a doctor."

> *Peg felt the same deep-down-to-the-bone fatigue that she'd always felt during fights with her ex-husband. As she listened to her brother repeat his rant into Sally's voicemail, Peg wished that she could curl up on the sofa cushions, close her eyes, and disappear.*

* * * * * *

When you're going through something intense with another person, it's all too easy to go into a metaphorical crouch. Like a dog jealously guarding a bone, your field of vision shrinks and you can see only danger. From this keyed up perspective, almost anything the other person does is going to register as an affront.

Notice, too, how this defensive posture is fed by the fight-flight-freeze reaction and the "autopilot" impulsivity that accompanies it. Both Gerry and Peg retreated into their old conflict habits, some of which had evolved in reaction to each other, in their growing up years, when they had lived under the same roof. Gerry's conflict habit was to gear up for a fight and to try to summon others to his cause. Peg, who was enervated by conflict, craved an escape from confrontation and began to disassociate.

Like their sister Sally, who had fled the scene, Gerry and Peg had been triggered into the human stress reaction. Notice that the three siblings' fight-flight-freeze reactions were not in response to any physical threat. All three underwent rapid neurochemical changes on account of an exchange of words. Language has this power—it can amp up existing tensions in the room, and also create new ones.

Here's something less obvious: It wasn't only the *intentions* behind the siblings' words that triggered the stress response. It was the specific way that each person in the room *interpreted* what was said that triggered him or her into a stress response.

It's worth lingering a moment on that last point. We are not only set off by something another person says to us. We are set off by what we *perceive* that other person to have said. Our physiological reactions are often a product of our own internal fears.

It follows, then, that whatever message Sally had been trying to convey to her brother and sister had less impact on them than their internal translations of that message. Each received the message through the filter of his or her preconceptions and anxieties.

When, in her frustration, Sally had blurted, "I might as well be Mom's only child," Gerry and Peg heard her telling them, *"You don't matter."*

When Sally said, "I'm the only one who gives a damn about [Mom's] well-being," Gerry and Peg heard her saying *"You're both shirkers who don't love or care for Mom the way you should."*

As Sally pressed her siblings to see things her way, Gerry heard Sally as arrogantly declaring herself the best and most informed of the siblings. Peg heard the same, and felt resentment at the thought of being judged by her sister, with whom she had often felt in competition.

Of course, in the heat of the exchange, none of the siblings could have sorted out their own interpretations so neatly. Instead, all three were temporarily incapacitated by the anger, shame, insecurity and pain that their words had managed to stimulate in each other.

Practice Pause

Think back on a recent interaction that resulted in you feeling disconnected from someone. Can you pinpoint the thought or interpretation that caused this?

THE 4 COMPONENTS OF COMMUNICATION

Imagine if you could have a transcript of every conflict that escalated out of your control. You could work backwards from the inferno to study the places where each person's words had been like gasoline on a campfire.

Even handier than a transcript would be a map that helped you avoid the tripwires in a sticky conversation as you navigated it. Or an "app" that reminded you of your earlier intention that you would *not* raise your voice to your teenager this time, but would instead try to model the kind of even-tempered exchange you wanted with him.

We actually use variations of all three of these tools in our Mediate Your Life trainings. We study and learn from past conflicts by reenacting them. We use the Mediate Your Life "maps" to prepare you to navigate future conflicts. And we show you how to design your own "apps," or built-in reminders to help you keep to your intentions about how you want to respond in a conflict situation.

At the very heart of our training are the 4 Components of Communication as identified by Nonviolent Communication (NVC). These components can help you think and talk in a way that is more likely to create good relationships.

The 4 Components are:

- **Observations**
- **Feelings**
- **Needs**
- **Requests**

The best way to understand the 4 Components is to see them in action.

In this example, a speaker uses **Observation, Feelings,** and **Needs** to think through and communicate something that he or she doesn't like. Then the speaker makes a **Request** to suggest a specific change.

> When you leave the house without saying good-bye (Observation),
> I feel <u>sad</u> and <u>lonely</u> (Feelings)
> because I really like having <u>companionship</u> in the mornings. (Need)
> Would you be willing to give me a kiss before you leave the house each day? (Request)

What's so savvy about using the 4 Components? Well, imagine if the sentences had instead come out this way, without them.

> When you blow me off each morning, (Ouch, Judgment)
> I feel rejected and abandoned ("Faux Feelings," or feeling with an accusing story attached)
> because I should not have to put up with your chilliness. (Judgment, with no need stated)
> When are you going to start being more loving? (Judgment, without a clear request)

See how radically language can shape our perceptions? Did you feel your body tense as you read the second set of sentences? You don't have to guess which language is more likely to produce a change in the person who is being addressed. The 4 Components help the speaker to stay clear-headed and also to stay in connection with the addressee.

Notice the deliberate caution and care of the **Observation** line. "When you leave the house without saying good-bye" is worlds apart from "When you blow me off each morning." The latter is a judgment that will make the listener angry and defensive and almost certainly closed off to whatever else you might say next.

In the first pair of sentences, the **Feelings** were "sad" and "lonely." Maybe the poet in you prefers the more dramatic adjectives "rejected" and "abandoned," but it's more effective to stick to the simplest feeling descriptions. That's because these can stay focused on what *you* are experiencing and do not implicate the other person.

Now let's examine the idea of the **Need.** "I really like having companionship in the mornings" also stays focused on you and something that you could imagine everybody wants in some form: companionship. (In another scenario, the need could turn out to be something else, like food, rest, ease, love, or play.) The alternative wording, "I shouldn't have to put up with your chilliness" hints at the speaker's need, but the need is buried and unnamed, even to the speaker. The energy is passive-aggressive, and more focused on reprimanding the other person than getting clear about the problem.

How will the other person respond? If he or she has managed to stay composed while taking in all the judgments of the second sentence pair, the question "When are you going to start being more loving?" may push him or her over the edge. It's not really a question; it's a demand that is at once hurtful and maddeningly vague. There's no do-able **Request** there. On the other hand, if the speaker asks, "Would you be willing to give me a kiss each day?" the request is perfectly clear. The other person also will not feel accused or punished by that request.

So, again, what's so savvy about the 4 Components of Communication? The magic is in how the 4 Components can put language to work for you. We've already established how language can be disconnecting. Language also shapes your reality. Case in point: If you start out thinking that someone is "a jerk," then odds are good that you'll experience that person that way. Starting with a judgment-free **Observation** can give you a clearer perspective on another person's actions, and can help you isolate the **Feelings** that arise in reaction to whatever it is you observe. Naming your feelings can help you can get clear about your **Needs.** And once you know exactly what you need, you can use **Requests** to ask for what you need in a non-accusatory way that gets results.

THE DISTINCTIONS THAT MAKE THE DIFFERENCE

Those who teach Nonviolent Communication frequently refer to the 4 Components of Communication as "OFNR," which you'll sometimes hear pronounced "OFF-ner." We'll try to resist making a cheesy joke about how much "off-ner" you'll like how your relationships are faring when you remember to use OFNR.

To use OFNR well, it's crucial that you be able to separate

Observations from **Judgments**;
Feelings from **Faux Feelings**;
Needs from **Strategies**;
Requests from **Demands**.

Here is a more in-depth explanation of each of the 4 Components, along with the *crucial language distinctions* that make them so effective.

<u>O</u>BSERVATION = stating what you have observed as the stimulus for your current experience.

Note the giant difference between observations and judgments. "I dropped the dish and it broke" is an observation; "I am an idiot who can't do anything right" is a judgment. When you make the distinction between observation and judgment, it creates a space for you to interpret the world differently.

Observation vs. Judgment
Judgment: "She is rude and mean."
Observation: "I don't like it when she teases me about my weight."

<u>FEELINGS</u> = the bodily sensations that arise in you as a result of having interpreted the stimulus in a certain way.

The key distinction here is between true feelings and what we call "faux feelings." (See Appendices A&B) The latter are adjectives that are often dubbed "feelings," but that are in fact telling a story about another person. For example, the statement "I feel betrayed," is really saying, "Someone betrayed me." Faux feelings include an interpretation of what someone else did to you (e.g., "I'm feeling annoyed/rejected/abandoned"). Feelings are descriptions of what is going on inside of you (e.g., "I'm feeling content/sad/lonely"). When you can distinguish between feelings and faux feelings, you can more accurately describe your own internal experience—which, in turn, allows you to more easily connect with others.

<u>Feeling vs. Faux Feeling</u>
Faux Feeling: "I'm feeling humiliated" (i.e., "She humiliated me.")
Feeling: "I'm feeling upset."

<u>NEEDS</u> = the universal human need that is met or not met at a particular moment.

Feelings are a terrific guide for helping you to locate an unmet need. Otherwise, you may confuse your need with a strategy. All of us have needs for food, rest, and shelter, and those can be fairly straightforward. The rest of our universal human needs can get more complicated. For example, you may experience a need for love, and believe that it "needs" to come from a particular person. Or you may say, "I need that job" when the job is in fact a reflection of your need for financial stability. When you can distinguish between needs and strategies, you increase the likelihood of getting your needs met, because you can see that a need can be met by any number of strategies.

Needs vs. Strategies
Strategy: "I want her to shut up and leave me alone."
Need: "I want <u>acceptance</u>. And <u>freedom</u> from judgments about my body."

REQUEST = asking for something specific and doable that will meet your unmet need.

Do you know how to ask for what you want? It's not as easy as it may seem. Maybe you have trouble getting specific or in naming what you *do* want, as opposed to what you don't. Maybe you bring a lot of "demand energy" to your requests. It's easy to slip and to say, "Can't you be more considerate?" instead of "Would you be willing to take the dog out for a walk?" When you can distinguish between requests and demands and be more specific in your requests, you will find that people are more open to what you propose. You may even find that they are delighted to know how they can contribute to your happiness.

Requests vs. Demands
Demand: "You have to stop teasing me and quit being such a jerk."
Request: "Would you be willing to stop making references to my body size? You may not mean anything by it, but it makes me feel uncomfortable all the same. I'd like it if you could find another way to connect with me. Can you think of something else that we could joke about together? You're a Yankees fan and I like the Red Sox. Could we joke with each other about that?"

A TOOL FOR LIVING UP TO YOUR INTENTIONS

Did you ever notice how much easier it is for a conflict to escalate with the people who are most important in our lives?

Even though they once had been close, the siblings' shared history created landmines in their communications. The fact that Sally was the "baby sister" made it difficult for her older brother and sister to let her take any sort of leadership role. They also tended to bristle at any implication that they were lacking compared to Sally. Although Gerry and Peg recognized these patterns in themselves and could even laugh about them, the old habits and accustomed family roles were hard to shake.

Even though all three siblings felt enormous affection for each other, it could be tricky for them to *hear* each other accurately. Whenever any one of them got mad or scared or stressed, that person inevitably interpreted what the other siblings said as a judgment or attack (or both).

Gerry had always had a slightly uneasy relationship with Sally, because, in their shared family of origin, she had been the "good kid" to his rebel. When he perceived Sally as questioning his commitment to their mother—the mother Sally claimed they might soon lose—this had touched a nerve. Reeling with anger and fear, Gerry had lashed out. His words had bubbled up and out like boiling water in a too-full spaghetti pot:

> *"Don't you think you're overstepping here? Just because you never moved away doesn't mean that you're in charge. Mom's still Mom. And she has other children besides just you."*

Sally had often felt insecure about how her brother regarded her. She had grown up feeling envious of Gerry and his un-self-conscious demeanor. She admired him for being bold enough to do whatever he wanted, and had once felt abashed by his observation, years ago, that Sally had become "the perfect suburban mom." In Sally's ears, Gerry's retort about her "overstepping" had sounded like this:

> "You're out-of-line. You never did anything interesting with your life and so it's absurd that you would see yourself as having any power or insight in this situation. I am dismissing what you've observed in Mom. And you are not as important as you think you are."

With that interpretation in her head, Sally shot back:

> "Mom's not still Mom. If you cared enough to come home more often, you would know that. And I might as well be Mom's only child, because I'm the only one who gives a damn about her well-being!"

In Gerry's ears, Sally's words sounded like this:

> "You're in denial about Mom and you are a bad son because you moved far away. You and Peg don't love Mom enough. I am the only one who is right and I am the only one who cares."

Imagine if Gerry or Sally could have had the presence of mind to recognize that they were both reacting from a space of defensiveness and anger. Imagine if just one of them had been able to absorb the other's speech, acknowledge that it had upset them, and then consciously choose to respond with care and curiosity about what the other person was going through.

In order to side-step our own worst interpretations, and to avoid escalating a conflict, it can be helpful to put our thoughts into what is sometimes called the OFNR "training wheel sentence":

When I see/hear you...
I feel....
Because I need...
Would you be willing...?

In response to Gerry's insistence that "Mom's still Mom" and his accusation that Sally was "overstepping," Sally might have used the OFNR formula to respond in this way:

> "When I hear you wondering if I'm 'overstepping' (Observation)
> I get <u>worried</u> (Feeling)
> because I really want <u>collaboration</u> in making any big family decision (Need)
> Would you be willing to tell me how I can better include you in this process of deciding what we'll do for Mom?" (Request)

Similarly, at the moment when Sally stormed out and slammed the door, Gerry or Peg might have gone after Sally and said:

> "When you raise your voice and slam the door (Observation),
> I feel <u>scared</u> and <u>upset</u> (Feelings)
> because of my needs for calm and predictability. (Needs).
> Would you be willing to come back in the house when you're ready and take just ten minutes to talk about what you are going through right now?" (Request)

The "training wheel sentence" is so named because it's akin to riding a very simple, very steady bike. It gets you started. It may feel stilted at first. But, for all its initial awkwardness, this formula will definitely help you to *get* clear and to *be* clear. In other words, using OFNR will help you to rapidly sort out the situation for yourself and then to communicate what you are experiencing to someone else without triggering that person into another fight-flight-freeze reaction.

Would Gerry have been disarmed if his sister had reinforced their sense of connection and checked in with him instead of going on the attack? Would Sally have found it possible to regain her calm more quickly if one of her siblings could have offered her the space and safety to do so? The answer is *yes*—at least eventually. Used well, the OFNR formula will absolutely dial down the intensity and dial up a sense of security for everyone involved. It becomes an open door to more (and more constructive) conversation.

> **Practice Pause**
> Think back on a recent interaction that escalated into conflict. Try using OFNR to express how you felt in that moment. "When you ____ [Observation], I feel ____ [Feeling], because I want ____ [Need]. Would you be willing to ____ [Request]?"

Sorting Through Different Realities, Focusing On The Now

Has something like this ever happened to you? Let's say that you are waiting in line to pay for your groceries, and it's taking longer than you would like. You feel irritation and think, "This checker's an idiot. What's his problem? Ugh, I'm going to be here all day!"

This is another instance in which you can transform what happens next by peeling back your judgments to reveal a simple observation.

When you translate "This checker's an idiot" (judgment) into "This checker is looking up codes for nearly all of the produce items" (Observation), the second statement alters your perception. You realize the guy at the cash register may be new on the job, or he may care about doing his job well. You may then feel a shift in yourself because your original, emotional reaction (impatience, irritation) was attached to a different *interpretation* of what was happening. This opens up many more options for how you can choose to respond. You are no longer at the mercy of your interpretation of what someone else says or does. Instead of acting annoyed or brusque when you get to the head of the line, you might be able to appreciate the care the checker shows as he handles your groceries. You might even feel moved to express this appreciation out loud, which could, in turn, shift the experiences of the checker and the people around you.

There's a refreshing clarity that arises from unwinding the emotional reactions in which we are often caught. This is true even when we get clear about something that is more difficult.

Suppose that you are in a slow-moving line in another store. This time, you see that the delay is caused by two store employees who are bantering with each other and paying scant attention to the shoppers who are attempting to pay for their purchases. In this scenario, you can quietly grouse about how "clueless" or "unprofessional" the two employees are being. Or you can use OFNR to make visible what you and the other shoppers may be experiencing.

> "Seeing you talking (Observation), I feel some reluctance (Feelings) to interrupt,
> but I'm feeling some urgency to complete here so I can get home to my family. (Need)
> Would you be willing to shift to checking me out?" (Request)

Would you be brave enough to say the above to the employees? There's actually nothing "brave" about the 4 Components of Communication. The only reason it might feel

Teach the kids this!

bold is because of cultural conditioning that tells us to avoid conflict and the repercussions resulting from raising an issue that might be interpreted as criticism.

For example, a shopper who was frustrated with the two distracted employees might have grown angry enough to say the following:

> "I can't believe how rude you are! Do you think we have nothing better to do than to listen to you two blather on to each other? It's like we're invisible. Give me the name of your manager, because somebody has to teach you how to show some respect."

Put yourselves in the heads of the employees. Which approach do you prefer? The careful, openhearted OFNR approach? Or the shaming, vindictive approach? The latter may be more common in our culture. But which language is more likely to help the employees be more clear about what the speaker wants and more interested in giving it to them?

We all may exist in the same objective reality, but each of us can only perceive that reality through our individual senses. Each human being has a different perception, a different point in the universe from which he or she interprets what happens. Our respective "realities" are therefore informed by our individual experiences.

An American adage that may date back to the Cherokee tribe of Native Americans says, "Never judge a person until you've walked a mile in their shoes." Each of us is carrying around our own sets of troubles and distractions. So it makes sense to treat each other with care, and to be curious about what might be causing a reaction or behavior in someone else that we don't like. All of us know that this is true. But oh, how challenging it can be to act on that knowledge when we're going through our own "something."

Learning how to stay curious about other people's realities and helping them to get curious about your own reality is the key to better relationships. If you can reliably model and evoke this kind of openhearted curiosity—which is also called "empathy"—then you'll have the power to crack open the most intractable conflicts.

Rabbi and family therapist Edwin Friedman once noted that *"In any situation, the person who can most accurately describe reality without laying blame will emerge as the leader, whether designated or not."* We've certainly found this to be true in our experience as mediators. It's also an insight that we've built into our trainings. The more mindfully you can use language to describe a perceived reality, the more likely you are to lead the way to resolution.

Often people in conflict stay stuck in their own interpretations. In their language and actions, they end up constantly reinforcing their distress and hurt.

Consider how thoroughly Gerry and Sally managed to misinterpret and over-interpret each other's remarks. When Gerry had dubbed Sally the "perfect suburban mom," he had intended it as a compliment of the orderly way in which she managed her family's schedule. Yet Sally had assumed he was making fun of her. And when Sally had tried to tell Gerry that he didn't have all the information he needed about their mother's health, Gerry thought that Sally was calling him out for being irresponsible. In fact, she had nothing of the sort in mind. She wanted to fill him in and she wanted to share her perspective.

Practice Pause
Think back on a moment when you were made unhappy by another person's actions. What happens when you attempt to describe what that person was doing in observation language, without reference to your emotional reactions?

Often, in conflict situation, people are remembering a reality that existed at some prior point in time and are arguing over what happened—or what they *perceived* to have happened—back then. This is essential to keep in mind when you're trying to resolve any conflict, but especially one that involves people who have any sort of history with one another.

Staying focused on the "now" of the conflict can also be valuable when you are having a reaction. If you find yourself not liking something, it helps to figure out exactly what has triggered you. By shifting out of judgment and into observation, you can begin to compare your reality with the reality of the other person.

Using the language of OFNR can sometimes feel like turning the key in a lock. Suddenly, the door swings open and you find you can move forward with the person with whom you were at an impasse. Even if you don't agree about your respective versions of what happened in the past, you each begin to open up to the possibility of shared understanding and resolution. That's because each person can trust that the other is person working to see his or her perspective. People tend to shift when they believe their versions of reality have been heard.

THE PSYCHOLOGICAL BENEFITS OF BEING HEARD

When we have a sense that someone has really gotten us, it can be quite cathartic and emotional. So much of the time, people feel lonely; we don't really get heard, and we also don't really hear others. That's why there is a deep satisfaction and a huge psychological relief that comes from being heard. There is a quiet intimacy to this experience that is like no other. We experience a sense of community and companionship, and gratitude that we are not all alone in the world.

* * * * * *

Sally knocked lightly, opened the door and slipped quietly back into the house. "I'm back. And I'm really sorry for leaving like I did."

O.

She kicked off her shoes and sat next to Peg on the sofa, wrapping her arms around her sister. "I'm scared, guys. This is even harder than when we lost Daddy, because, you know, we had Mom to be in charge then. When I see Mom looking so thin and vulnerable in that hospital, and when she starts asking me the same questions over and over...." Sally trailed off a moment before continuing. "I've been saying that I just want to keep her safe. If I'm honest, I want someone to keep me safe, too. Would you guys be okay if we wait until tomorrow to talk more about what we'll do for Mom? Because I could really use some rest and quiet tonight. We haven't been here together in a long time—"

F:

N:

R:

Gerry broke in, "Why do you keep saying that?"

Sally smiled. "Because I miss you. Because I'm so glad that we're together now."

Peg laughed, "Yeah, why can't you deal with the fact that your two sisters are crazy-happy to see you, Ger?"

"I love both of you guys so, so much," whispered Sally, as her voice started to break. "So let's take a pause from all the serious stuff tonight and try to have some fun together so we can feel like a family again." Sally sat up straighter. "Can you maybe tell me what you just heard me say?"

"I believe you just said that I'm your favorite brother," offered Gerry.

Peg shot a sofa cushion at him. "Sally just told us that she could use a break. This stuff with Mom is heavy. She's been the closest to it lately and it's scary as hell. Sally needs our support."

"You are supportive! You both are." Sally's voice again began to quake. "I just need to know that things are still good with us."

"We're here for you, Sal." Gerry said gently. "We love you, too."

Sally started to cry. Then her phone beeped, indicating that she had a new message. She looked at Gerry with a confused expression on her face.

"You sent me a voicemail?"

Gerry winced. "You can delete that. Please don't listen to it. It isn't relevant and, anyway, I was being stupid. It isn't how I feel anymore."

Practice Pause

Take a closer look at Sally's words above. Can you locate the 4 Components in her words? What was her Observation? What were her Feelings? Her Needs? What Requests did she make of her siblings?

THE IMPORTANCE OF PRACTICE

It's one thing to understand the 4 Components of Communication and quite another to use them "in the wild," or in your everyday life. Don't get discouraged if, when you first try to use OFNR, you aren't as clear as you thought or if it's all too easy to lapse back into your old conflict habits.

The best way to improve at using the 4 Components is to commit to practicing them through conflict role-plays. You can certainly review OFNR in your own head, but there's nothing like a practice dialog to help you to realize, say, that sorting out the difference between a "need" and a "strategy" can be quite challenging in the heat of the moment. In the next chapters focusing on the 4 Components, we will give techniques that will help you get into practice with each Component and give you a starting point for your practice dialogues.

We recommend four different ways to practice the concepts outlined in this chapter and in the rest of this book.

1. Focused practice with a partner, using the techniques in the next chapters;
2. Empathy with a partner: talk about real situations and use the techniques to parse out the 4 Components in what your partner says;
3. Empathy with a group;
4. Practice "in the wild" (in everyday life).

NEXT UP

It's surprisingly easy to mistake a judgment for an observation. Differentiating between the two requires reflection and practice. In the next chapter, we give you some handy techniques to make the process easier.

3 | What Actually Happened?
Observation Versus Judgment

"To observe without evaluating is the highest form of intelligence."
-J. Krishnamurti

A slow smile crept over Maggie's face as she knocked the mud from her soccer cleats and clambered into the backseat. A delicious aroma had enveloped her as she opened the door to the minivan. "Dad-dy! You got Chinese take-out again. Mom's going to be so mad!"

"Not true," said James. "I got your mother a double order of eggrolls. She can have them when she's back from Grandma's tonight."

"But she spent so much time making the lasagna in the freezer. She's going to flip out when she finds out we didn't eat it."

"Come off it, Mags." Maggie's older brother Corey was slumped in the front seat with his eyes glued to his phone. "You know Mom and Dad were fighting too much this morning to remember to defrost anything. That lasagna is solid ice."

James glanced with surprise at his son. "That's right, it is. But we weren't fighting." He shifted uncomfortably, remembering the disagreement with Sally. When his wife had asked him to attend the meeting with Corey's guidance counselor, James had objected to taking the time off from work. "I can't continue making all these sacrifices," he had complained. "You may enjoy being taken advantage of, but I don't. Get Peg to look in on your mom for once."

"You think <u>you're</u> making sacrifices?" Sally had sputtered.

"Well, yeah. It's not reasonable to think I can drop everything for a daytime parent-teacher meeting. You know my job isn't casual like yours is."

"My job is 'casual'?"

"Flexible. Oh, don't make a big deal of it. Your job is flexible. Mine isn't."

Sally's voice had dropped. "I'm going to make an observation." Her mouth moved slowly, as if she were chewing on something that tasted bad. "When I hear you say that you 'can't keep making sacrifices,' I feel....amazed. I feel amazed that you could be so selfish and so clueless!"

* * * * * *

In the midst of a confrontation, it's easy to feel convinced that your perception is the truth. Of course your partner is being inconsiderate! The teenager who sasses you is definitely a spoiled brat! Your boss is undoubtedly a fool when he criticizes your work!

As you know from the previous chapter, our initial reactions typically spring from our interpretations of the situation at hand. As humans, we inevitably develop stories that explain the things that are happening around us. Sometimes these stories serve us. In moments of conflict, however, they can be a serious impediment to understanding. That's why, until you learn to separate judgments from observations, you will remain stuck in your story.

The first half of this chapter will explain in more depth the difference, or distinction, between an observation and a judgment. The second half of the chapter will share four techniques that you can use to support others to distinguish between observations and judgments. We'll also touch on how you can practice making this distinction in your own mind when you find yourself stuck in judgments and evaluations.

OBSERVATIONS VS. JUDGMENTS

There's a world of difference between an observation and a judgment. But most of us make the leap from observation to judgment with enormous ease. Consider the following pairs of sentences, which illustrate this leap.

Observation: She kept looking at her watch during our conversation.
Judgment: She doesn't like spending time with me.

Observation: He told me to re-write two sections of the report.
Judgment: He hates my work.

An observation is your perception of what occurred. It describes what you witnessed in language that doesn't include your reactions to or interpretations of what happened.

A judgment is an interpretation of what happened; it's the story that your mind creates in response to something that you have just seen or heard.

If someone kept looking at her watch while you were together, that could perhaps signify distraction or disinterest. But drawing the conclusion that the person doesn't like spending time with you is an interpretation. Perhaps the woman who kept looking at her watch was worried about losing track of time, because she had been running late to her appointments all day. Perhaps she was hungry and looking forward to dinner. It may be that she was enjoying her time with you, and didn't think to explain her frequent time-checks because she didn't know that they were causing you discomfort.

Similarly, the person who asked you to re-write two sections of the report could hold any number of opinions of your work. It may be that his request for revisions was intended in the spirit of collaboration. It may be that he was quite pleased with the rest of the report, but wanted to help make those two sections even clearer and stronger.

Locating Observations—Inside And Out

Judgments can be serious impediments to understanding, especially in moments of conflict. Until you learn to separate judgments from observations, you will remain "stuck in your story"—with your vision clouded by your own interpretations.

So how do you peel back judgments to get to the observation? One way to do this is to try to imagine the scene as a camera would have recorded it.

Let's use the example of the supervisor who asks you to re-do two sections of a report. Imagine that you leave the meeting feeling upset and hurt. When a coworker asks you what happened, you offer your judgment: "He criticized my report." This is an interpretation of what happened. If we had a video recording of the meeting, it might show your boss saying, "I would like the report to be clearer about the purpose of the project. How about if you re-write these two sections to do that?" Returning to this statement gets you closer to the observation. It also helps you get clearer as you consider the actions you will take next.

Your choices from moment to moment are inevitably influenced by your thoughts. That's why, in separating observations from judgments, it can be helpful to bring forward whatever is happening inside of you—your thoughts and sensations—and make it a part of the *internal* observation. So, when your coworker asks what happened in the meeting with your boss, you could say, "I'm having the thought that he criticized my report." This statement is itself an observation of what is happening for you internally in the present moment. It describes your *reaction* to the words that your boss spoke.

(Note that finding the internal observation requires you to

take on a witnessing role to your own inner state. Some people have more experience doing this than others. Regardless of how familiar this is to you, it is a skill that you strengthen with practice.)

Locating external and internal observations will help you shift out of the judgments that may be blinkering your perspective. It also will give you more space between whatever it is that has happened and your reaction to it. In that space, you can regain presence and create more connection with those around you.

Practice Pause

Think of a recent interaction and how you interpreted it. See if you can locate both an external observation and an internal observation.

The Wisdom Of Communicating With Observations

When you align what you say with your observations, you reduce the chances your communication will go "off the rails." Carefully speaking in observations instead of with judgments can help ensure that the other person hears what you want them to hear, so your message does not get distorted by the other person's interpretations.

Beginning a conversation with a judgment tends to be self-defeating. If the judgment is about the other person, he or she is likely to interpret your words as a criticism, and, *boom!*, you will find yourself in a conflict over whether the criticism is true.

Getting back to the scenario with the workplace report, let's imagine that you wanted to talk to your boss about his feedback. If you open the conversation with, "I'd like to talk to you about how you criticized my report," the rest of what you want to say may be lost because your boss may react to the judgment. If, instead, you open with, "I'd like to talk to you about your request that I re-do two sections of the report," you are more likely to be able to continue.

A second non-judgmental way to begin a conversation with your boss is by sharing your internal experience: "I had the impression yesterday that you were critical of my report." By stating it this way, you "own" your interpretation of what your boss said, rather than declaring it as a truth. Again, this approach can help you increase the likelihood that you and your boss will have a clear and satisfying exchange.

Bottom line: Begin with an observation—not a judgment—if you want the rest of what you have to say to be heard.

Let's consider the morning quarrel between James and Sally over who would go to their son's parent-teacher conference. We don't know how Sally worded her request that James attend. We do know that James responded to that request with a few different judgments—and that these judgments quickly created friction between the couple.

> James: *I can't continue making all these sacrifices. You may enjoy being taken advantage of, but I don't. Get Peg to look in on your mom for once.*
> Sally: *You think you're making sacrifices?*

Notice how Sally tossed back an implicit judgment of her own; i.e., that James' sacrifices were insignificant compared to her own. James then responded with a defensive statement about the nature of his job and how it restricted his choices. The conflict ramped up and up as both James and Sally continued speaking exclusively out of judgments fueled by their negative interpretations of the other person's words.

James: *Well, yeah. It's not reasonable to think I can drop everything for a daytime parent-teacher meeting. You know my job isn't casual like yours is.*
Sally: *My job is 'casual'?*
James: *Flexible. Oh, don't make a big deal of it. Your job is flexible. Mine isn't.*

Was that last statement an observation? Not exactly—at least not in the context of a conversation that James and Sally were having. Opening with a judgment had made it impossible for either of them to accurately hear what the other might be trying to say. It also sent their stress levels into the stratosphere, and neither was able to respond rationally. Sally attempted to use OFNR, but she was too much in the grip of the fight-flight-freeze response to follow through on her attempt to locate the observation.

Sally: *I'm going to make an observation. When I hear you say that you 'can't keep making sacrifices,' I feel....amazed. I feel amazed that you could be so selfish and so clueless!*

By this point, both James and Sally were upset and angry. (Little wonder that no one remembered to take that lasagna out of the freezer.) They would both need a cooling-off period before they could make another attempt at clear communication and connection.

Suppose the morning conversation had unfolded differently. Suppose James had responded to his wife's initial request with an observation instead of a judgment. That might have allowed Sally to respond in kind.

James: *I already have several appointments and deadlines scheduled this week. I don't see how I can do all that and leave work early.*

Sally: *I promised to help get Mom's house ready for Gerry's visit. I've missed so much work already since her last hospital stay. I get nervous about falling even farther behind at work if I have to fit in the appointment with Corey's teacher.*

They may not have found a resolution yet, but already the conversation is going better. Sally has even inserted an internal observation about her thoughts and feelings. This might invite James to do some of the same.

James: *It sounds as if we both have packed schedules. I want to be helpful to you, and I am also feeling a lot of dread and worry at the thought of trying to miss work at this time of year. I think my colleagues and my boss would not appreciate it. I wonder if there is another way I can help support your mom and alleviate some of your stress without my having to leave work early? For example, could we ask to reschedule the teacher meeting for after my regular work hours?*

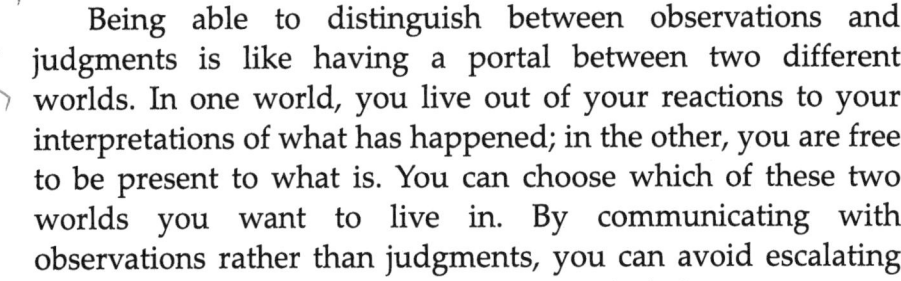

Being able to distinguish between observations and judgments is like having a portal between two different worlds. In one world, you live out of your reactions to your interpretations of what has happened; in the other, you are free to be present to what is. You can choose which of these two worlds you want to live in. By communicating with observations rather than judgments, you can avoid escalating the conflicts that we all experience in our daily lives.

> **Practice Pause**
> Think of a recent interaction that ecalated into a conflict. Can you recall the judgments that took you out of connection with the other person?

WHAT HAPPENS WHEN WE LET GO OF JUDGMENTS

In many cases, we experience conflict because we are holding judgments about another person. Once you start believing that the other person is being difficult, rigid, impossible, or narrow-minded, it will be nearly impossible for you to truly hear anything that he or she tries to say. Once you believe that a conflict is intractable, it will likely become so.

You can also trip yourself up in a conflict situation by holding judgments about yourself. For example, you may start to tell yourself that you shouldn't have entered into the situation, that you should have seen it coming, or that you should know better how to deal with it. All of these judgments will increase your sense of overwhelm and keep you locked in a recurring state of fight-flight-freeze.

To gain greater clarity regarding the conflict you're experiencing, you might need help stepping outside the story in your head. You can ask another person to help you get clear about exactly what happened that prompted you to interpret events as you did.

You can also offer to help another person who is mired in his or her interpretations. Often it is easier to help another person to distinguish between observations and judgments than it is to do this for yourself. This is especially true when you are in the thick of an escalating conflict.

her story/version

* * * * * *

Right after the morning argument with James, Sally was still feeling jangled and irritable. "He always looks out for himself," Sally fretted. "Why does James always put work before any of us?"

Sally noticed her use of "always," which was one red flag that she was stuck in her judgments. She recalled a time when the kids were small and when Maggie used to come to her to complain about her brother.

"Corey is being mean to me!" Maggie would wail.

"What is Corey doing that you see as mean?" Sally would ask.

"He won't give me a turn on the tire swing."

"Why do you think he is doing that?"

"Because he is mean!"

Sally sighed at the memory, because she was stuck in a similar looping pattern of blame. She had the thought that James was selfish when he did not agree to alter his schedule to relieve some of her own scheduling pressures. She also hadn't liked it today when he referred to her job as "casual." She had become so angry about his word choice and his allusion to "sacrifices" she couldn't follow through on her attempt to get to an observation. She instead blurted her interpretation, which was that James was both selfish and clueless.

Sally suddenly felt a pang of regret at having lashed out. "Now why did I say that?" she wondered aloud. "I didn't really mean it. Honestly, it felt kind of good to say those words in the heat of the moment. But judging James didn't get me where I wanted to go at all."

* * * * * *

In our work, we've noticed that when someone shifts his or her attention from a judgment to an observation, that person experiences a physiological shift.

Notice what happens to your own bodily sensations when you read these sentence pairs:

Judgment: "He came in and yelled at me!"
Observation: "He came in and spoke louder to me than I liked."

Judgment: "She nagged me about chores."
Observation: "She asked me if I would take out the trash."

Did you notice your breathing change from one sentence to another? A simple rephrasing can begin a shift inside you, and you will literally feel it in your body. This shift can help establish or reestablish a connection between two people.

Even if you are not working as a formal mediator, you can begin to mediate your own and others' conflicts by zeroing in on the observation.

Sally's memory of helping her daughter separate judgments from observations ended up allowing Sally to do the same for her own conflict with James. Getting the support that helps you get to the observation can be essential—even for people who are practiced at it.

TECHNIQUES FOR FINDING THE OBSERVATION

In our trainings, we ask our participants to practice the following four techniques for supporting others to get clear in the midst of conflict. Each technique offers a slightly different way of responding to what someone else says, gently nudging him or her to separate their interpretation of events from what actually happened.

TECHNIQUE #1: PURE REFLECTION

The first technique is simply to reflect back what someone else says, including their judgments. We do not recommend doing this as part of empathizing with somebody unless combined with other techniques below, but we find it a valuable technique to practice as it helps you learn to stay focused on the other person. You can either literally use the exact same words they have used, or you can reflect back your understanding of what they said, using your own words. The idea is to stay focused intently on the other person, without offering any advice and without telling them your opinion. The goal of this technique is to demonstrate that you are hearing the person as he or she would like to be heard.

Your job is to keep saying what you're hearing as your practice partner tells a story. But "saying what you're hearing" does not mean that you will simply be a parrot. (Even though it may feel that way at first.) You don't have to limit your reflections to observations and judgments. You might also include what you hear someone to be feeling, needing, or requesting.

Try working on this technique with a practice partner, and see if you can reflect back what your partner says seven times in row. The repetition may feel a bit silly at first, but stick with it. It will help you to build the habit of reflecting.

Your practice session might sound something like this:

Partner: "I just had a meeting with the most unpleasant people."
You: "OK, you had a meeting with some unpleasant people."
Partner: "Yes! They were horrible. I've never met such a negative bunch."
You: "They were horrible and negative?"
Partner: "Then I got out of the meeting and my boss started treating me unfairly."

You: "After the meeting your boss did some things which were unfair to you?"

Partner: "Yes! He told me I have to work this weekend."

You: "And he told you that you have to work this weekend?"

Partner: "Yeah, now I'm going to have to cancel the plans I had with my son."

You: "Ah, you had plans with your son that you can't go through with now."

TECHNIQUE #2: SEPARATING OBSERVATION FROM JUDGMENT

The second technique asks you to take the first step in separating observations and interpretations. Your job is to peel back the other person's judgment to get to the "camcorder" version of what happened. Often, the simplest way to point out the judgment is to insert a qualifying statement when reflecting the judgment, such as, "You're thinking that..." or "As you see it..."

Use the examples below to begin practicing with your partner:

Partner: "I'm so stupid! I can't believe I said that to him."

You: "So, you're telling yourself that you're stupid for saying what you said?"

Partner: "He is treating me unfairly."

You: "Oh, as you see it, he is treating you unfairly?"

Partner: "I just had a meeting with the most unpleasant people!"

You: "You had a meeting with group of people that seemed to you to be very unpleasant?"

TECHNIQUE #3: GUESSING THE OBSERVATION

The third technique lets you help someone differentiate between observations and judgments in yet another way. When you know some of the context behind the person's judgments, you can make a guess about what the observation might be. By taking a guess at what is prompting your partner to have a certain judgment, you can help your partner focus on what actually happened.

Review these examples as starting points for your own exploration:

Partner: "He is treating me unfairly."
You: "Do you feel that way because of something he said during the staff meeting?"

Partner: "I just had a meeting with the most unpleasant people!"
You: "Were you bothered by how they talked over one another during the meeting?"
Partner: "No, they were just rude! They didn't listen to any of my proposals, I don't know why they bothered to bring me in at all."
You: "Oh, so is it that your proposals weren't received the way you would like, and they went ahead with something else?"

Notice how even a wrong guess can still help you and your partner get closer to the observation. The trick is to keep listening intently, so you can be prepared to offer another guess that will help your partner get clear about what happened.

TECHNIQUE #4: ASKING FOR THE OBSERVATION

If you don't have enough information to guess the observation, you can simply ask for it. This is the fourth technique.

Check out these examples:

Partner: "He is treating me unfairly."
You: "What is it that he said or did that is unfair?"

Partner: "I just had a meeting with the most unpleasant people!"
You: "What about them did you find unpleasant?
Partner: "They were just rude! They didn't listen to any of my proposals, I don't know why they bothered to bring me in at all."
You: "What happened when you made a proposal?"

FOR FURTHER PRACTICE

Once you and your practice partner have each had a turn with the four techniques above, ask your partner to talk about a real-life situation about which he or she has judgments. Use any or all of the four techniques to support your partner to find the observation behind those judgments. Remember if you use the first technique of pure reflection to think of it as a place to start, reflecting judgments so your partner knows you are paying attention and hearing her on her own terms. Then shift to the other techniques to support your partner to find the observation.

Remember to switch roles and repeat. Afterward, talk to each other about how you each feel about your respective situations. Notice which techniques felt most comfortable to you as the support partner, and which techniques best supported you when speaking about your real-life situation.

Practice Pause
Take a moment to think about how you could use the four techniques above to help you to separate your own judgments from observations.

HELPING OTHERS GET TO THE OBSERVATION

Have you ever called up a trusted friend to vent? Maybe there is someone in your life whom you trust to listen to you at your most uncensored. You can share your gripes with this person without being afraid that this person will be turned off or will stop liking you.

Sometimes this trusted person might be you. Maybe you have a friend or friends who know they can call on you to listen when they're really frustrated or mad about something.

It can feel good—and also a little daunting—to be the friend who listens. You want to offer the other person solace, but what is the best way to do that? Do you just listen quietly or do you vocalize a shared indignation at what the friend is going through? What if you get the sense that your friend might not be seeing the whole picture? How can you best be supportive then?

Used well, the four observation techniques can be extremely useful in being the kind of friend that we all would like to have—the one who offers unconditional acceptance, while also supporting us out of our fight-flight-freeze reactions.

After the difficult morning exchange with her husband, Sally and her siblings, Gerry and Peg, also had a conversation that escalated into conflict. The conflict got so heated that Sally slammed the door and fled the house. Feeling torn up, she had phoned her friend Alicia, who was practiced in NVC mediation.

As you read this transcript of their conversation, see if you can notice the judgments in Sally's statements. Then notice which of the observation-finding techniques that Alicia chooses in her replies.

Sally: *Why is this happening to my family? We're falling apart.* [handwritten: Judgement]

Alicia: *It sounds as if you're having a day where you're feeling pretty disconnected from everybody, is that right?* [handwritten: #2]

Sally: *Yes. And that's because everybody's saying the stupidest things to me today.*

Alicia: *What are some of the things that sound stupid to your ears?* [handwritten: #4]

Sally: *(laughing a little) Well, James told me that my job's a joke, for one thing.*

Alicia: *Did he use those words to describe your job— "a joke"?* [handwritten: #4]

Sally: *No, no. He didn't use exactly that word. He called it "casual." Said I had more flexibility because my job is "casual."*

Alicia: *He said your job was "casual."* [handwritten: #1]

Sally: *Yeah, then he corrected himself and said he meant to say "flexible." We were arguing about the parent-teacher conference and he was being super stubborn.*

Alicia: *Ah, you two were arguing about which of you would have to go to the conference and you were thinking he was being super stubborn?* [handwritten: #3]

Sally: *Yeah, he doesn't want to go. Says it's hard for him to get away from work. Which I know is kind of true. Oh! And he also said something about how he's making all the sacrifices in our family. That topped the list of stupid things people have said to me today.*

Alicia: *James said that he is making all the sacrifices in your family?* [handwritten: #3]

Sally: *He said something about how I might be fine with making sacrifices, but he was done with that.*

Alicia: *What do you think James meant by that?*

Sally: *Well, the next thing out of his mouth was that I should get Peg to help more with Mom. That made me angry, but, if I'm honest, I've been saying the same thing to James all winter.*

Alicia: *So when James said that he wanted more help from Peg, you think that he was repeating something that you've also said?*

Sally: *Well, sort of. I feel horrible even saying this, but it would be great to get back to something like "normal" with Mom's situation. I just keep waiting for the other shoe to drop, you know? First Mom broke her shoulder when she slipped on her back stairs. Then came the incident with her driver's exam. Then the Senior Center calls to tell me that they think Mom's showing signs of dementia. And now this latest scare with her heart. It's been a crazy winter, and I haven't been able to be around as much as I used to be for James and the kids. James has been picking up some of the balls that I'm dropping.*

Alicia: *Your life is changing because your mother has been needing you a lot lately. And that's having an effect on your family.*

Sally: *Yes, that might be it. (voice breaking) And now that we're talking about Mom, I can't even begin to tell you how mad my brother made me just now.*

Alicia: *You're brother made you extremely angry right before you called me?*

Sally: *Gerry hasn't been in the country for 24 hours, but he's already decided that I'm Chicken Little and everything's just hunky-dory with Mom continuing to live on her own.*

Alicia: *Oh, so it sounds like he might be seeing the opposite of what you're seeing.*

Sally: *We're completely at odds.*

Alicia: *You and Gerry really can't see eye-to-eye on this yet. But I'm guessing you and Peg must have more of a shared reality around what your mother might need?*

Sally: *Oh, don't get me started. Peg was just like a deer in headlights once Gerry started talking.*

Alicia: *Peg didn't react in the way that you would have wanted. She was...quieter than you would have liked?*

Sally: *Oh, you know Peg. She gets really passive whenever there's a disagreement.*

Alicia: *Peg gets silent and withdrawn when there's a fight?*

Sally: *All she could say is that she wants us to let Mom decide everything.*

Alicia: *Peg wants your mother to make decisions about her own care.*

Sally: *Yeah. And of course we all want that. But we also have to be realistic.*

Alicia: *You and Peg and Ger all agree that you want your mom to have input. But you in particular want something else, too. You want...some sort of shared understanding around what your mother needs?*

Sally: *(starting to sob) I do want that. I also want... simplicity. Maybe I also want some more predictability? It's all about safety. Keeping Mom safe. Keeping her happy. And keeping her family intact.*

Alicia: *Right now you're feeling like things aren't simple or predictable? You're feeling like things aren't safe?*

Sally: *That's right. Because it's not safe! All it would take is one pot left on the stove or one slip in the bathroom. I'm on tenterhooks all the time and this is looking like a long journey ahead. The last thing I need is Gerry fighting me all the way. And I don't want to be unreasonable about Peg—she works so hard and she really does try—but I could really use a little acknowledgment from her right now.*

Alicia: *It sounds like you're feeling scared and overwhelmed right now. I wonder if you might need some support and rest.*

Closes with the need

Through her guesses and questions, Alicia supported Sally to locate the observations that had sparked all her judgments. Once Sally was in touch with the observations, she found herself feeling calmer and more clear-headed, so she had more options for how to respond.

> **Practice Pause**
> Think of a judgment you hold of someone else, and see if you can find the observation. Consider enlisting a practice partner to help.

NEXT UP

What comes after you've located the observation? You move on to the next of the 4 Components of Communication. In the next chapter, we discuss feelings and how to separate feelings from faux feelings.

4
How Do You Feel About What Happened?
Finding Feelings

> "So when you are listening to somebody, completely,
> attentively, then you are listening not only to the
> words, but also to the feeling of what is being
> conveyed, to the whole of it, not part of it."
> —J. Krishnamurti

Alicia grinned at the sound of her son's car pulling up out front. Ben had recently landed his first "real" teaching job and gotten his own apartment. But he and his mother still kept up their longstanding tradition of Tuesday taco night.

"How's everybody's favorite teacher today?" Alicia called out as Ben entered the kitchen. Ben laughed, but without his usual gusto. As he set to work making the guacamole, Alicia could see a hint of dejection in her son's posture.

"Ben, I'm curious about what might be going on for you. Did you have a rough day?

"Oh, Mom. It'll be fine. I just had a problem with this one kid who decided to challenge me in front of my sophomore English Lit class." Ben shook his head.

"Challenge you how? What happened?"

"It shouldn't have been such a big deal. The kid has been acting funny in class—spacing out, making little side comments under his breath, you know? So I asked him to sit in front. He moved really slowly, to show me he didn't like it. Then he sat down and shoved in his earbuds."

For a split second, Alicia looked confused. "At first, I thought you said 'earplugs.' You mean he put on a pair of the little stringy things that all the kids use to listen to music."

"Listen to music or tune out the people they don't want to deal with, yeah. This kid came down front and put in his earbuds the exact moment I started talking. It was ridiculous. Of course, all the other students started laughing. And I got mad."

"You were angry?"

"Yeah, and I could have handled it better than I did. But it had already been a long day, and I felt so disrespected. I felt like this kid was trying to undermine me."

"You felt embarrassed?"

"Embarrassed, sure. And surprised that things could go downhill so quickly." Ben sighed and managed a wan smile. "It's days like this that make me wonder if I'm really cut out for teaching."

* * * * * *

"How are you?" You might ask this question—and answer it—a dozen times each day. "Fine," you say. "I'm fine." The answer may pop out of your mouth without much thinking behind it: "I'm-fine-how-are-*you*?"

The exchange of "How are yous?" may seem like an empty ritual, especially if it appears that no one is really listening for an answer. But the question is intended to show recognition and care, even between strangers. It points to the importance of feelings as a tool for connection. Inquiring about another person's internal state—or searching for non-verbal clues that reveal the same—is the quickest way to relate to another person's experience.

Feelings convey important information. Cross-cultural researchers such as Paul Ekman have identified a small number of feelings that can be conveyed through universally recognizable human facial expressions. The list includes expressions of sadness, happiness, anger, surprise, disgust, and fear. But what about other types of feelings? We have so many different words to describe them, and they come in many more shades than the short list above.

Some feeling words attempt to describe bodily sensations, or to name whatever physical state is being produced by the release of neurotransmitters and hormones in the body. Putting language to these internal, physiological phenomena is the only way to bridge the inherent gap between yourself and others. It gives others a way to empathize with what you tell them you're going through by comparing it to experiences of their own.

Feelings also reveal whether or not your universal human needs are being met. But you can easily hide that information, even from yourself, if you are unaware of the flow of your feelings and of how to access them. Knowing how to recognize and talk with others about feelings will bring you a cascade of benefits, including the inner calm that comes from self-knowledge and much greater connection with the people in your life.

This chapter will teach you to discern between feelings and "faux feelings," which are evaluations that masquerade as feelings. It offers three techniques for translating faux feelings into the actual feelings that will help you to better understand your experience and will allow you to communicate more clearly, especially in conflict situations.

Practice Pause
What are you feeling right now?
Write down at least two adjectives that sum up your answer.

FEELINGS VS. FAUX FEELINGS

Most of us are not taught to be fluent in the language of feelings. That's why it is so commonplace to end up talking instead about "faux feelings," which are the thoughts and evaluations that substitute for feelings. Think of this category of "faux" or "fake" feelings as a layer of evaluation or judgment. Very often, you have to sift through this layer in order to get to the real feeling or feelings buried below.

As you read this, you may be wondering, "How could anything that is as personal as a feeling ever be fake?" The "faux feelings" we're talking about are adjectives that may initially sound like feelings, but are actually stories about what the speaker perceives outside of himself or herself.

For example, suppose a friend tells you that she is "feeling threatened." That phrase tells you about the situation in which she has found herself. Something potentially dangerous is going on, and you'll want to take your friend's words seriously. But the word "threatened" is, in fact, in the category of faux feeling because it does not tell you about your friend's *internal* emotions. What she is actually feeling inside may be a mix of fear, sadness, panic, and anger. The difference between feeling and faux feeling matters, because you will attend to your friend's fear in one way and to her experience of being threatened in quite another. (The former might involve lots of empathy and being present for her, and the latter might involve helping her move to a secure location and contacting law enforcement.)

Some examples of **faux feelings**:
abandoned, attacked, betrayed, forgotten,
mistreated, misunderstood, taken-for-granted

Some examples of **feelings**:
frustrated, sad, scared, overwhelmed, peaceful,
playful, affectionate, interested, joyful

(See Appendices A and B for full lists of feelings and faux feelings.)

In a conflict situation, it is essential to sort out feelings from faux feelings. This is not only because you'll respond to each differently, but also because the language of faux feelings is often an obstacle to resolving a conflict.

Notice how Alicia managed to make guesses about Ben's feelings just by observing his face and body language. She deduced that her normally exuberant son was feeling "dejected." "Dejected" is a feeling and it is a word that seemed accurately to capture Ben's internal experience by the end of the school day. As he relayed the events of the day to his mother, he was feeling sad and discouraged.

What had Ben been feeling at the moment of the conflict with the student? Ben used the words "disrespected" and "undermined." These are examples of faux feelings, which is not to say that they are wrong or unimportant. But "disrespected" and "undermined" carry an implicit judgment of someone else. They sum up Ben's evaluation of what was being done to him. They suggest that he may have been feeling embarrassed, hurt, resentful, angry, frustrated, or disappointed, but without any specificity. All the listener can be sure of is Ben's judgments about the events.

Alicia listened carefully to Ben's story. When he shared an actual feeling, she reflected that. She also gently speculated out loud about the actual feelings that might be submerged beneath the faux feelings.

Ben: *All the other students started laughing. And I got mad.*
Alicia: *You were angry?*
Ben: *I felt so disrespected. I felt like this kid was trying to undermine me.*
Alicia: *You felt embarrassed?*

"I feel abused" or "I feel misunderstood" are a few more examples of faux feelings. Again, we are not dismissing these statements by calling them "faux." But we are calling attention to the fact that they are evaluations. When someone says, "I feel abandoned," he is really saying, "Someone has abandoned me." As the listener, you could use empathy to inquire after the person's actual feelings. It could be that he is feeling sad, afraid, or hurt, or a combination of all those things.

Faux feelings often manage to camouflage two or more actual feelings, and it is the actual feelings that contain the real insights about how to proceed with a conflict. That's one reason that Alicia sought to translate her son's faux feelings into the actual feelings that could help him more. When Ben said he was feeling "undermined" by the student with the earbuds, Alicia guessed that he might be feeling embarrassed. Ben confirmed that this was true. As he had sensed things going "downhill" in the classroom, Ben had also been feeling scared and alone. With that information, he could make a clearer choice about what to do next.

From a grammatical standpoint, true feelings words are used only to describe a state of being, which is itself a reaction to whether your basic human needs are met or not met. When you talk about feeling happy or sad or nervous or excited, you're describing a sensation or neurochemical reaction that is emanating from within you. A true feeling word contains no allusion to something that is being done to you by another person. It's solely about what's going on inside of you at a particular moment in time.

When you put your focus on a bodily sensation and then name it, you are naming an experience that other people can relate to. Most everyone knows what "afraid" or "confident" feels like, because these emotions are universal. When a friend tells you she is "overjoyed," you know at once what she means, because you have your own reference points that allow you to understand her experiences. That is why, when you want to share what is going on for you, talking about your feelings is often more effective than talking about your evaluations, judgments, thoughts, or stories about the situation. Peel back the layer of faux feelings, and use the language of feelings to help you find out what is really going on inside of yourself and others.

Practice Pause

Review what you wrote down earlier about how you were feeling. Is your answer a feeling or a faux feeling?

FEELINGS IN CONFLICT SITUATIONS

When people are in conflict, they are often reluctant to reveal emotions. Showing feeling can seem akin to showing weakness, or something to be avoided at all cost. Our culture reinforces the assumption that sharing feelings is risky. In some settings, showing emotions is equated with immaturity, unprofessionalism, or irrationality. In light of these realities, the person who gets teary or whose voice breaks during a fight may indeed be put at a social disadvantage. Signaling that you are upset or in pain can invite harassment or exclusion from others who are frightened by those emotions.

So learning to bury your feelings can *seem* like a good choice—even and especially when you are in a conflict with someone you know well. But there's a big problem with that strategy. When you have strong feelings that you don't express, you will almost always come across as guarded and defensive. If you are trying hard to hide the fact that you are feeling hurt, uncertain, afraid, or insecure, you will do so from a place that other people will read as aggressive, arrogant, aloof or condescending.

When you find yourself in a place of emotional withholding and reflexive self-protection, it's extremely common to start substituting evaluations for feelings. Vocalizing these "faux feelings" can create an abrupt disconnection, even if you were trying to find your way toward a connection.

For instance, have you ever been in a meeting and heard someone say, "I feel belittled," or "I'm feeling disrespected"? The effect in the room is palpable, as people's pulses quicken and their breathing becomes shallower. You'll see people literally withdraw and contract with self-protective body language. For the moment at least, they have become less receptive and open to others. This certainly happens in the person being addressed—who is implicitly being criticized before the group—and it also happens to the speaker, who is in touch with a faux feeling rather than an actual one. It's hard to overstate the detrimental power of a faux feeling. Because those around you will hear them as judgments, faux feelings only add more fuel to the fire of conflict.

Locking down your feelings can feed the fight-flight-freeze response, which happens to be contagious. The tension you're feeling will transfer to others, and they will likely respond in kind, without fully understanding why.

Although it may seem counterintuitive, you have much more power in a conflict when you are able to reveal a true feeling. Doing so can generate a surprising amount of tenderness and connection between people who were mired in conflict just minutes before. When you're aware of your own feelings and are able to take responsibility for them, other people will soften and relate what you've shared to something in their own lives. You'll both have more choice about how you will respond to each other, and will move in the direction of a resolution.

> **Practice Pause**
> Think of a recent conflict and how you felt during it. Scan the feelings list (Appendix A) to find the feelings that matched your internal experience. What might have been different about the conflict if you had known you were having those feelings or had shared them out loud?

* * * * * *

Ben spotted Corey sitting outside the guidance counselor's office. He gestured to the boy to take out his ear buds. "Hey, Corey, I'm sorry I got so angry in class yesterday."

"Oh," Corey looked at the ground. "No big deal. I didn't even remember it until now."

"Well, it was kind of a big deal to me. I went home and felt terrible about it. I even talked to my mom about it."

Corey looked up again, his eyes wide.

Ben chuckled. "Yeah, teachers have moms. How about that?"

Corey laughed self-consciously. "Yeah, I know that."

"I didn't use your name or anything. I never do. We were talking mostly about how I reacted in class and it made me realize that I should level with you about how I was feeling."

After another nervous laugh from Corey, Ben went on. "I love teaching. I've been volunteering in classrooms for a long time. But this is my very first year at your school and, although I don't like to admit it, sometimes I'm scared."

Corey snorted. "Scared of what?"

Ben took a deep breath before he spoke again. "Scared because it's a brand-new school. Scared that I won't be the kind of teacher I want to be. I don't like feeling scared, but it happens sometimes. I also feel embarrassed and worried when I'm anything less than perfect in front of my students."

"My mom says nobody's perfect."

"Your mom is right. But I still feel embarrassed and worried. Especially when I do something stupid, like blow my top at a student just because he would rather listen to his music than to me."

"Is that why you were so mad, Mr. Loewen?"

"Well, yeah! Didn't I say that?"

"You said you were tired of me 'making a show of how bored I am.' But I wasn't bored. I think what we're doing in class is pretty cool. I just don't like being in front of people."

"But you put in your ear buds right when I started talking."

"I swear I wasn't even thinking when I did that. It's just a habit. I don't even have music on most of the time. But people think I do, and that lets me be invisible."

Corey let his gaze drop to his feet again. Ben stared, speechless, at the top of the boy's head. Several seconds passed as he processed what Corey had just said.

"Wow. I'm really glad you told me that. But, Corey—why do you want to be invisible?"

The guidance counselor stuck her head out of the doorway. "Cor, we're ready for you now."

Corey stood up. "Gotta go."

Ben put a palm on Corey's shoulder. "What's it like for you here at school? Why do you want to be invisible?"

"It's just easier, y'know?" Corey shrugged and turned to go. Then he took a step back. "Maybe I'm embarrassed and worried all the time, too."

Ben grinned. "Well, that makes two of us. And where there are two, there are probably more. Maybe we'll form a club."

Corey rolled his eyes, and then smiled in spite of himself. "Yeah, maybe. See ya later, Mr. Loewen."

Techniques For Finding The Feeling

Feelings arise, even when cultural messages tell us that they're not acceptable. The cautious and indirect ways that we refer to our feelings in these situations can confuse our communications, creating more disconnect.

The following techniques are designed to help you notice the ways that others may unconsciously "muddy the waters" when talking about feelings. The three techniques will help you discern the other person's actual feelings.

You'll notice in the sample exchanges below that we don't encourage you to ask: "What are you feeling?" That's because most people are inured to that question and rarely answer it directly. You'll get much farther if you instead make a guess about what the other person is feeling. For example, "Are you feeling frustrated?" is an invitation to share that a frustrated person will often accept. Even a wrong guess can be useful, because it may prompt a response that brings both you and the other person to greater clarity. (E.g., "No, I'm not feeling frustrated, but I am feeling sad and disappointed.")

Technique #5: Translating Faux Feelings

Very often, you'll find that people use words that they think are feeling words, but that actually imply that someone else is wronging them in some way. These are the "faux feelings." Translating another person's faux feelings into real feelings can allow that person to get in touch with the emotion behind a judgment. This helps you both to get clearer about the other person's internal experience in the present moment.

There are many ways to translate faux feelings, as shown by the alternative phrasings offered below. (Perhaps you and your practice partner will add a few more.)

Partner: "I feel criticized."
You: "When you say that, are you feeling angry?"
—Or—
You: "Is that the same as saying you're angry?"
—Or—
You: "Are you upset about that?"

Partner: "He betrayed me!"
You: "Were you hurt by what happened?"
—Or—
You: "Are you feeling hurt about that?"
—Or—
You: "Are you hurting?"

Partner: "I feel unloved."
You: "When you say you feel unloved, are you sad?"
—Or—
You: "Are you bummed about that?
—Or—
You: "Unloved? Are you frustrated?

Partner: "I'm being harassed at work."
You: "Are you frightened about how you are being treated?"
—Or—
You: "Is that scary?"
—Or—
You: "Are you angry about that?"

TECHNIQUE #6: TRANSLATING IMAGES

Some people communicate metaphorically, using an image to convey how they feel. Certain images are fairly unmistakable, and you don't need to translate them out loud. For example, if someone tells you, "I feel like a mountain lake at dawn," you can be pretty sure that the person is feeling calm and serene and you only need to say that out loud if you think it will aid your connection. At other times, however, the other person's image-metaphor may be ambiguous, and so it may be important to confirm its meaning. This double-checking will often help the other person get even clearer about whatever he is trying to express.

EXAMPLES:

Partner: "I feel like a comic bombing during a standup routine."
You: "Are you saying that you are feeling embarrassed?"
—Or—
You: "Are you embarrassed?"
—Or—
You: "Is that like being really insecure?"

Partner: "I feel like a child lost in the woods."
You: "When you say that, are you feeling scared and lonely?"

Partner: "I'm like a bomb getting ready to explode and make a big mess."
You: "When you feel that way, are you angry?"

Partner: "I feel like a mountain lake at dawn."
You: "So you are calm and serene?"

Partner: "I'm like an explorer getting ready to set off into the unknown!"
You: "Does that feel adventurous and exciting, or are you nervous and worried?"

TECHNIQUE #7 TRANSLATING THOUGHTS

People frequently frame their thoughts as feelings, and this can easily muddle the two. This is, in part, a pitfall of our language. In English, you can say, "I feel like..." or "I feel that..." and what comes next can be a thought or opinion instead of a feeling.

If you can substitute "I think" for "I feel" at the beginning of a sentence about how you feel, then what you are describing is not a feeling. For instance, you can't substitute "I think angry" for "I feel angry." That's because angry is a true feeling. On the other hand, "I feel like I am not welcome there" could indeed become "I think I am not welcome there." That's how you know that you are stating a thought rather than a feeling, and this awareness can prompt you to inquire into what you feel internally, perhaps angry, bewildered, or sad.

There's nothing inherently bad about using "I feel" when you share a thought. However, in certain situations, this construction can inadvertently create disconnection and so it's useful to be aware of that. Supporting the other person to translate a thought into a feeling can help you both connect more easily. It will help the other person get clearer about how she is feeling, and it will help her to know that you are listening carefully.

EXAMPLES:

Partner: "I feel like he does not understand me."
You: "Are you distressed about this?"

Partner: "I feel that they really don't appreciate me at work."
You: "When you say that, do you feel discouraged?"

Partner: "I feel like there's no place that I belong."
You: "Are you feeling insecure and afraid?"

For Further Practice

To practice Techniques #5-7 above, have your partner think of a situation (real or imagined) as the basis for a starter sentence. E.g., "I feel manipulated" (Translating Faux Feelings), or "I feel like a dog being driven to the vet" (Translating Images), or "I feel like my coworkers see me as an outsider" (Translating Thoughts). Carefully choose your response. Your partner can either continue with their example, or move on to a new one. Switch roles after each technique so you both get experience empathizing with a partner who is using feelings. Try talking about your real feelings once you feel confident in your ability to use these techniques. Make sure you leave time at the end of your practice to reflect with each other on how the experience of using these techniques was for each of you.

Finding Your Own Feelings

While speaking with Corey outside the guidance counselor's office, Ben inadvertently helped Corey get to a feeling. This happened after Ben had openly shared and claimed responsibility for his own feelings, rather than blaming them on Corey or anyone else.

You may have noticed that separating faux feelings from feelings is much like separating evaluations from observations. When you recognize that you are substituting a faux feeling for an actual feeling, you can also remind yourself to separate out the observation (i.e., whatever happened that led to the evaluation). Then try to isolate the feeling behind that evaluation.

It's so useful to have a practice partner to support you in sorting out feelings. With continued practice, you can also get pretty good at supporting yourself through the process. Chapter 2 imagined what might have happened if Gerry had the capacity to separate observations from evaluations after the disagreement with his sister, Sally. To recover from his fight-flight-freeze reaction after he and Sally had quarreled and Sally slammed the door, Gerry could have focused on his feelings in the aftermath of the fight. Here is what that process might have looked like:

Gerry stalked out to the backyard and continued to pace. "That was horrible. Who does Sally think she is? I feel so totally insulted." Gerry caught himself. "Wait. 'Insulted' is not really a feeling. So, what am I actually feeling when I say I'm feeling insulted? I guess I'm angry. I've been agitated ever since Sally started hammering her point about how I don't know what's going on with Mom. That must have been why I was feeling so belittled?"

Gerry stays on that thought for a few minutes, initially unaware that "belittled" is a faux feeling. Then he reflects, "I could say 'I THINK that she was belittling me,' so that's also not a feeling. That's an evaluation. (Boy, this is tough.) Okay, so if that's a faux feeling, what is it that I'm really feeling about the stuff that Sally said?"

Gerry felt his mind draw a blank, so he checked in with his body to see if that could help. He noticed some tension in his chest, and an unpleasant fluttering in his stomach.

Suddenly, it hit him. "I guess I feel scared. I'm anxious about helping my mom and my sisters through this new challenge, especially so soon after we lost Dad. Now I'm also feeling sad. And both those feelings are triggering my habitual way of responding in situations like this, which is to try to hide any sense of weakness and to be willing to fight."

Gerry stopped pacing. He stuffed his hands in his pockets and looked down at his shoes.

"I'm afraid that what Sally was saying will be true, and that I'm not going to be able to handle it." He heard himself choke back a sob, but willed himself to stay with the *sensation of fear and sadness, and found himself wondering if Sally was feeling the same. "I don't really know if Sally was belittling me or not. Maybe we're both just handling a tricky situation in the best way that we can. I'm a little confused about that, so maybe I could talk to Sally later about what was going on for her."*

After a moment of feeling good about that decision, Gerry resumed his reflection. "Regardless of what was going on with Sally earlier, I also really want to talk to Mom and her doctor about Mom's prognosis. I feel like I'm being drafted into a war, but I have no idea what the battle is for." Gerry felt a surge of energy in his body, and then noticed that he had used a metaphor instead of a feeling.

"So how would a drafted soldier who doesn't have enough information about the war feel? I'm frustrated. I'm also feeling helpless and discouraged about being told what to do, without having as much control as I would like. Then again, just having gotten in touch with what I'm really feeling, I'm more hopeful. Now I'm curious to see what might happen with some more conversation." Gerry pulled his hands from his pockets and walked back toward the house, pleased at how much more open and relaxed he now felt.

Notice how Gerry began to step out of his "story" — or his judgments about Sally and her motives. Putting yourself a short distance from your story gives you the space to regard it anew. Just as it is helpful to focus on the observation instead of your judgment, noticing what you are actually feeling can help you create an internal shift that changes everything for the better.

NEXT UP

Once you know what you are feeling, it is helpful to know *why* you are feeling it. Our feelings arise because our needs are either met or not. In the next chapter we'll look closely at what needs are and how they connect us with others.

5 | What's the Underlying Motivation?
Finding Needs

"If the other person's behavior is not in harmony with my own needs, the more I empathize with them and their needs, the more likely I am to get my own needs met."
—Marshall Rosenberg

Peg kissed the top of her mother's head as her mother drifted back to sleep. Sally and Gerry were still sitting in the visitors' waiting room, where they had just finished their meeting with the hospital social worker.

"I knew home-care would be expensive, but those numbers are ridiculous," Gerry huffed.

Sally nodded grimly. "James and I have been talking about this for a while. The only way we can get the funds to cover a home aide would be for Mom to sell her place."

Peg slid into a chair beside her sister. "Mom would hate it if she had to move."

Gerry looked intently at Sally. "That old house is never going to fetch more than it does now. Are you saying that you and James would be okay with Mom moving in with you?"

Peg cleared her throat, "Actually, I had a better idea. What if I move in with Mom?"

"Oh, Peg!" Sally reached out to put her hand on top of her sister's. "We can't let you turn your life upside down like that. Also, that wouldn't solve the problem of paying for the home aide."

"Sure, it would," Peg insisted. "Mom would have me to help her instead."

Sally looked alarmed. She opened her mouth to argue, then thought better of it and looked at her brother in desperation. "Gerry?"

"I'm probably with Sally on this one, Peg." Gerry's tone was gentle. "She and James have a plenty of room and they'll soon have more, once Corey graduates."

"Corey!" Sally jumped to her feet in a panic and began rummaging for her keys. "Sorry, guys. I'll be back in about an hour. I'm late for a meeting at Corey's school."

Gerry raised an eyebrow in mock disapproval. "So you're running out on us again?"

"No!" Sally giggled uncomfortably. "Well, yes I am. But it's your nephew's fault this time." She stooped a moment to press her face to her sister's cheek. "Let's talk more about your idea later, Peg. Maybe the three of us can talk when I get back, ok?"

"Or maybe Gerry and I can keep on talking about it right now," Peg's reply had ice in it. "It's not like you have to supervise us every single minute, Sal."

* * * * * *

Many people are socialized to think they shouldn't have any "needs" beyond the very basics. Maybe you were trained to focus on the needs of others and not on your own. Maybe you worry that even talking about your needs somehow makes you "needy."

To get past these cultural constructs, take a minute to consider this question: What does every human being on the planet need to live a rich and thriving life?

Obviously, every human being requires air, water, shelter, safety, and sustenance. But beyond our common needs for survival, all of us, no matter where we live in the world, also share many other needs, including the needs for love, companionship, respect, autonomy, touch, connection, and a way to contribute. (See Appendix C for a full list of needs.)

In previous chapters, we talked about observations versus judgments and feelings versus faux feelings. This chapter will focus on the distinction between needs and strategies. It also will cover the crucial role that needs play in resolving conflicts, and will present four techniques to help you uncover the needs that may be obscured by a strategy. The chapter concludes with a discussion of how you can become more aware of the needs that motivate your actions and how you can use an awareness of your own and others' needs to improve all your communications.

Practice Pause
What need or needs of yours are being met in this moment?
What need is not being met?

NEEDS VS. STRATEGIES

Think of needs as those essential qualities that human beings need to survive and thrive. Just as humans need enough water to stay hydrated so, too, do they need intangibles such as touch and love and play for optimal physical and mental health. The needs covered in this chapter are universal in that every person on the planet will understand what it feels like to have these needs be met or unmet.

Strategies are the things you do and the actions you take to try to meet a universal human need. One example of a strategy is a cell phone. You don't need one, but owning one may be your strategy to meet the need to connect with others. Similarly, if your car helps you get back and forth to work, it might be your strategy for meeting the need for security. For someone else, that same car might be a strategy for meeting needs for freedom or for intimacy.

Just as certain turns of phrase in the English language can trip us up when we try to talk about our real feelings, so, too, can the language around "need" muddy the discussion of needs versus strategies. When someone says, "I need you to come home before dark," or "I need that delivery before noon," the things the speaker is asking for are not universal needs. Instead, the speaker is voicing strategies to meet underlying needs, perhaps for safety or predictability.

Since we aren't generally taught to be aware of our needs, each of us attaches our own images and meanings to the unmet needs that we (consciously or consciously) experience every moment of the day. Each person has his or her own strategies for making sure these needs are met. It can be extremely easy to get caught up in your strategies, instead of focusing on the needs that motivate them. So here's a tip: Strategies are specific, needs are non-specific. Humans can meet any need in a variety of ways.

For example, consider the myriad strategies out there to meet the basic need for food. Each part of the world has its specialty dishes. One group revels in hot spice, another in garlic-infused cuisine, and yet another in dining on snails or tripe. These are different strategies for meeting the same universal needs for sustenance. (Not to mention the needs for community, creativity, and a sense of belonging that can be met by food culture and eating-as-ritual.) There is usually no conflict between the guy who eats snails and the guy who prefers liver. They simply have different strategies for meeting a shared need to nourish the body.

When you can uncover the needs that your particular strategies are seeking to meet, then you can begin to locate the strategies that will satisfy the needs of everyone involved in a conflict. By translating what you say, or what you hear others say, into the universal needs that you or another person are seeking to meet, what seemed like an awkward impasse can recede into almost nothing. Consider Ben's surprise, in the previous chapter, when Corey explained that his ear buds weren't intended to show disdain for his teacher, but were his strategy to meet a need for "invisibility" or safety. Once Corey shared that information, teacher and student were no longer in conflict. In fact, being aware of each other's needs had brought them closer together.

Practice Pause
Choose a need from the list in Appendix C and then name up to three strategies that you could adopt to meet that need.

NEEDS IN CONFLICT SITUATIONS

Getting to the underlying needs can build a bridge between people when they are either in a conflict or are drifting toward one. Sally had been caught off guard when Peg offered to move in with their mother and become her aide. Sally immediately disliked the idea, because (she would realize much later) it did not meet her own needs for peace of mind and a sense of control. When Sally attempted to ignore her own needs by adopting an "other-directed" approach (*"We can't let you turn your life upside down like that."*), this only created more tension between the sisters. Peg felt irritated both by the language that appeared to deny her any choice in the matter (*"We can't let you..."*) and by what she perceived as Sally's disregard for Peg's needs.

When you find yourself in conflict with another person, it's likely that you have conflicting strategies. You may feel certain that your need will not be met unless your strategy prevails. Sally had a strategy in mind for how her mother could be absorbed into Sally's household and she believed it met everyone's needs. Peg, however, saw this plan as robbing their mother of her autonomy. Peg's desire to move back into their mother's house and to manage her care was a strategy for preserving her mother's independence. She also knew it would meet her own needs for shelter, community, and security.

As long as the two sisters stayed focused on their respective strategies, they would remain in conflict. The way forward, therefore, was to discover their underlying needs and to talk openly about them. Was there a way that each sister could yet meet her needs through strategies that did not compete? Importantly, was there a strategy that could meet their needs and all of their mother's needs, too?

The heart of the "needs" approach to conflict resolution is to bring people's motivations to the surface and to name the needs behind our strategies. When you can loosen your grip on your strategies to focus on the "why" behind those strategies, your whole relationship to the conflict can begin to shift.

Keep this approach in mind. It will support you the next time you are working through one of the small, daily conflicts that arise with those closest to you.

Practice Pause

Think about a conflict from your own life or that you've read about in the news. What are the conflicting strategies? What are the universal needs that each side is trying to meet?

---

* * * * * *

Sally and James had reconciled over a plate of re-heated eggrolls. Sally told her husband about the initial blowup with her siblings and the more connecting conversation that had followed. James told Sally about the surprise that had awaited him when he had stopped by the house that afternoon.

It was Thursday, the day that Corey and Maggie both had sports practice until late. Both kids were planning to take the late bus, because their mother was having her meeting with Aunt Peg and Uncle Ger about how to help Grandma Doris.

James felt vaguely disorientated as he stepped into the unaccustomed silence of the family kitchen. Was this yawning quiet what he and his wife had to look forward to in their "empty nest" years? He winced at the image of his own children trying to take care of him and Sally some day. Pushing the thought firmly out of mind, he continued with the task that had brought him home, and flipped impatiently through the day's mail.

Finally, he had found what he was looking for: a manila envelope from Corey's high school. James tore open the flap and felt his jaw grow tense as he skimmed the report. It was as bad as his son's guidance counselor had said. Worse even.

Just then, Corey padded downstairs in his sweatpants, a computer game console in one hand. The boy froze when he spotted his dad. After a beat, father and son had spoken in unison: "WHAT ARE YOU DOING HERE?"

James stared at his son in disbelief. "What am I doing here? Why are you not at cross-country practice?"

"I thought you'd be at Grandma's with Mom."

"THAT IS NOT AN ANSWER TO MY QUESTION!" James bellowed, slamming his hand against the table so hard that Corey flinched.

"And how do you explain this?" James held up the report card.

Corey glared. "So now you're opening my mail?"

"Two Ds and an F!" James voice started to break, which made him angrier.

"Don't freak, Dad." Corey wrinkled his nose. "It's just a mid-term report. It doesn't mean anything."

"Doesn't mean anything?" James snorted. "Do you think this is a joke? Lousy grades have consequences, Corey! Do you think that life is one of your stupid computer games, where you get as many do-overs as you want?"

James' sarcastic blow had landed. He saw his son's face contort with hurt and humiliation. Then it was gone, buried beneath a stony mask of defiance.

"You don't have a clue, Dad." Corey's voice was rising as he ran back to his room. "Why can't you and everybody else just leave me alone?"

GETTING CALM ENOUGH TO FIND THE NEEDS

Both James and Corey were reacting out of the stress response, which is much like going down an Olympic toboggan run. Once father and son pushed off from the top of the hill, they were on a swift and slippery path to the bottom. Their only options were to crash or to ride it out.

James and Corey's conflict came on abruptly, as a result of the report card and their ill-timed encounter. But there were other elements at play—namely, the conflict habits that parent and child established with each other over a lifetime of disagreements, big and small. This meant Corey and James really had two things working against them: Their individual fight-flight-freeze survival reactions *and* their established conflict habits, which can feel as irreversible as that hurtling toboggan.

So what could they do to jolt their cognitive faculties back into working order? When you're in a state of emotional overwhelm, how in the world can you locate the underlying needs that will help you connect with yourself and the other person? How do you avoid reverting to shouting, sarcasm, belittling, eye rolling, or any other irresistible conflict habit?

Research shows that just the simple act of becoming aware of the feeling (rage, fright, shame) that you are feeling reduces the external physiological measurements of that emotion. Simply *naming* and *feeling* your feelings in any given moment profoundly affects your experience of the situation.

We use this phenomenon all the time in our Mediate Your Life trainings, when we ask our participants first to isolate the conflict "trigger" and then to focus on what happens to them, physiologically, when the trigger is delivered. Focusing attention on the process allows us to release our focus on the stimulus, which, in turn, can free us from getting launched into a fight-flight-freeze reaction. Redirecting our attention in this way can literally shift us from survival to sanity.

* * * * * *

James fought the urge to follow his son. When he heard Corey slam the bedroom door, it took every ounce of willpower for James not to go bounding up the stairs to kick that door down. For Corey, the terrible report card "doesn't mean anything?" James was so angry he could hardly see straight.

He knew what Sally would have said if she had been there: "Just because your teenager is calling you to a fight doesn't mean you have to accept the invitation. Give yourself a minute to deal with what he triggered in you just now."

(James also knew what would have been his defensive retort, "This isn't MY problem. It's his. That kid needs to know he's acting like a jerk.")

After a few seconds of restless pacing, James started to climb the stairs. Again, he could imagine how Sally might have quietly re-directed him with observations and empathy. "You want Corey to know that it's not okay to fail out of school and to be rude. You also are still boiling mad. Are you sure you're ready to talk to Corey? Is what you're able to say right now going to create the outcome you want?"

James sighed. Family life had changed a lot since Sally had started her Mediate Your Life training. Initially, James had been resistant. Now he had to concede that Sally's example was improving the way he argued with the kids, even when Sally wasn't there. No, he wasn't ready to talk to Corey just yet. James went back downstairs, flopped back the couch, and attempted the "get-your-brain-back" self-connection exercise that Sally was always recommending to him.

What It Means To Self-Connect

The fight or flight reaction typically brings on moralistic thinking and "enemy images," in which another person becomes the unequivocal "bad guy." When you're feeling this disconnected from another person, the most helpful thing you can do is to check your connection with yourself and to "self-connect."

What does it mean to be "self-connected?" Self-connection brings a type of clear-headedness and resolve that comes from knowing what your needs are in the present moment. Even if a need is not met (a sufficient night's sleep, for instance), just acknowledging that you're tired and are wanting rest creates an experience of self-connection.

As James struggled against his desire to dash up the stairs to confront Corey, he saw that he was still in destructive mode. This meant he was likely to say and do things that would make the existing conflict worse. At another time in his life, James might have charged upstairs anyway, determined to "teach the kid a lesson" and to show Corey just how furious he was at him. Yelling could be gratifying—at least in the short term. Even anticipating his later regrets would not have stopped James from giving in to his overwhelming instinct to combat.

But now James knew another, more efficient way of facing his anger head-on. Using self-connection, he could calm himself and sort out the underlying needs that were causing the tensions with his son.

* * * * * *

Although he wasn't yet ready to admit it, James knew that yelling that was a lousy strategy, unlikely to ever meet his un-met needs. But yelling was the only strategy he had to meet his need for...what exactly?

James shut his eyes and noticed the tingling in his chest. A throbbing in his right temple. He was mad. Well, mad and stressed. And disrespected! Okay, so that might be a faux feeling, but so what? The 16-year-old had told him that he "didn't have a clue!"

Breathe in. Breathe out.

What were the underlying needs? Sally was so much better at figuring out these things.

He was mad and stressed because he needed respect, right? Sally always translated his hunger for respect into a need "to be heard," "to be seen," and "to matter" in Corey's life.

James had scoffed the first time she said that, but the tears that stung his eyes told him she was right.

There was another feeling in the mix. Fear. Corey's strange new behaviors were scaring James. So the powerful urge to "ground that boy for life" probably pointed to needs for "safety" and "predictability" regarding Corey's future.

James sat up straight again and opened his eyes. Was it possible that Corey was feeling some of this same fear as well?

THE POWER OF IDENTIFYING NEEDS

Part of what makes getting to the needs so powerful is also the biggest mystery of the conflict resolution process: the *ah-ha* moment when someone's perspective shifts. When you are in the thick of a conflict, your vision can get distorted by the stories in your head. It's almost like spiking a high fever brought on by the intense emotions that come out of your evaluations or faux feelings or frustrated strategies.

But once you can identify the needs behind your strategies, there is a moment of glorious, instantaneous insight, when fever subsides, your vision returns, and you can understand what the conflict is really about. All at once, you see more accurately what is motivating both you and the other person.

Farewell to the story about the other person being controlling and mean or cold and uncaring. All of a sudden, you really get that this person is trying to protect himself, or to take care of his family. You can see the need that motivates his actions.

You also can see the "why" behind your own behaviors. Instead of holding onto your strategy with a life-or-death grip, you realize that what you really need is some respect, or autonomy, or understanding. In this instant when your perspective shifts, you can shift out of the surface-level details, the story, the history and all that comes with it, and into another level—a level where you can see that the other person is just trying to meet his or her needs rather than to do you harm.

When you reach this shift in perspective, you do not let go of the stories or the judgments—*they let go of you*. The thoughts that were making you so miserable no longer have you in their grip.

James recalled exactly this kind of shift taking place in his daughter Maggie, back when she was just four-years-old. She had been walking home from the fireworks display with her friend Emma and their respective families. At one point, Maggie had asked Emma to hold her hand and Emma had refused. When Maggie started to cry, Sally had said to her, "Why don't you ask Emma why she doesn't want to hold your hand?" Maggie did as her mother suggested. "Why don't you want to hold my hand, Emma?" she asked. To which Emma replied, "My hand is cold. I want to keep it in my pocket."

Once Maggie realized why Emma was saying no, her face lit up as she experienced the shift. Maggie had seemed to think that Emma was refusing to hold her hand because she didn't like her and was rejecting her. Once she was aware that Emma just needed to keep herself warm, the old story in Maggie's head was gone, and she no longer felt upset. She asked Emma if she could link arms with her, and Emma said yes. In this way, the two girls found a solution through which Emma's need for warmth and Maggie's need for closeness were both met.

Remembering Maggie's "shift" reminded James to get curious about Corey's needs as well as his own, because this was the formula for reestablishing a connection. It was only from a place of connection that James and Cory would be able to find the strategies that could satisfy everyone's unmet needs.

* * * * * *

James still felt too upset about the report card to engage with Corey right away. But he was able to feel a softness toward his son that he hadn't been feeling a few minutes before. They would talk more later, maybe with Sally's help. For now, they could surprise Maggie by picking her up right when her soccer practice ended.

"Corey, I need you to come down here." Then he corrected himself, imagining how that sentence could have sounded to his son. "Corey, I don't want to talk about the report card just yet. Or about why you skipped practice today. But I would like to know what's going on with you, when you're ready to talk about it. For now, would you be willing to keep me company as I go pick up Maggie?"

Slowly, Corey's door opened and the boy stepped into the hall.

Techniques For Finding The Need

People often mix up their needs with their strategies. They do this in four primary way: by linking their needs to a person, place, thing, or time. Then they turn that person, place, need or time into a strategy that obstructs the underlying need. The four techniques below will demonstrate how this happens and also how to translate a strategy into a need. See if you can guess the need, or motivation, behind each strategy.

Technique #8: Disconnecting Needs From A Person

How often do you use the word "need" with this construction: "I need you to..."? What follows can be anything from "...take out the trash" to "...love me." The difficulty with this colloquial expression is that the other person may hear it as a demand. And why not? "I need you to..." is a perfect example of how needs and strategies get conflated. In this instance, the strategy is pretty bald: to try to get a need met by having someone else do a specific thing.

When you say, "I need you to...," it sends the message that your well-being is tied up in another person's actions. When you hear, "I need you to...," you get the message that the speaker's well-being relies on your doing what the other person says.

In either case, the implication is that saying "no" is not an option. Closing down on this freedom sets up an internal conflict for the person who has been singled out to fulfill the need.

This is easily interpreted as not really having any choice in the matter. If you don't appear to have the freedom to say no, this may stimulate your need for autonomy. You may end up in an internal conflict, torn between wanting to do what the other person has asked and wanting to do something else, just so you can assert your independence.

By separating a need from a specific person, it becomes possible to see that there are multiple options for getting our need met. If you still choose to ask a particular person to do something for you, having the spaciousness of knowing that you have other ways of meeting your needs often will make it easier for the person to hear your request and do what you ask. The same is true when you hear the "I need you..." construction from someone else. It's so much easier to comprehend the other person's fundamental need when it is uncoupled from any particular strategy. If the underlying need isn't clear, go ahead and make a guess, because, even if you've guessed incorrectly, this will invite the other person to clarify.

EXAMPLES:

Partner: "I need her to respect me."
You: "So respect is the key thing for you in this situation?"

Partner: "My boss needs to recognize the work I've done on this project."
You: "Would you like acknowledgment for the work you've done and, in particular, would you like it from your boss?"

Partner: "The kids should really pick up after themselves."
You: "Is it cleanliness that is important to you, or is it more about consideration?"
—Or—
You: "Would you like to have support around keeping the house neat?"

Partner: "He needs to take out the trash!"

You: "Are you saying that you want help with the household chores?"

—Or—

You: "Do you want more help with the household chores, or is it about shared responsibility for you?"

Technique #9: Disconnecting Needs from Places

Probably you feel some strong ties to particular places, whether they are places you've grown up, had meaningful experiences, or are just places you associate with doing certain activities. Perhaps you've had to say good-bye to a long-cherished home and have felt emotionally torn-up by the relocation.

When you get attached to a place in this way, you can begin to regard that place as essential to meeting your needs. In this case, you may have conflated the place with safety, care, and your personal well-being.

If you can separate your needs from the place, it broadens your possibilities and options. You can reflect on what it is about that particular place that is important to you, and consider whether or not there's another place that would equally meet your needs. This is not about being unsentimental. It's about increasing the opportunities for getting your needs met.

Examples:

Partner: "I need to be at my office."

You: "Are you saying that, if you were at the office, you would feel more confident about having all the resources you need to complete the project?"

—Or—

You: "Would being at the office help you focus?"

Partner: "I have to go to my friend's party."

You: "Are you looking forward to the connection and community?"

—Or—

You: "Will going help you experience some fun?

Partner: "I'm so bummed that I won't get to attend the meditation retreat."

You: "Were you looking forward to solitude?"

Partner: "Yes, but, more than that, I love the land at the retreat center."

You: "So is part of it about being connected to nature?"

TECHNIQUE #10: DISCONNECTING NEEDS FROM THINGS

Perhaps you can remember a time in your life when it seemed like having something—a new car, a nice house, or the latest tech tool—was the most important thing. Maybe you even felt as if your happiness depended on getting it.

Learning to disconnect needs from things is a helpful tool in our consumerist society, so that you can feel more choice and less compulsion to buy things. When you can separate the strategy of getting a new shiny toy from the need that you want the toy to fulfill, it frees you to consider what need you actually are trying to meet, and what strategies might be more likely to lead to what you really want. Shifting the conversation to focus on what is behind the strategy, and what will be satisfied by that strategy, opens the conversation for more mutual consideration of the best strategy to meet those needs. These strategies might even be far less expensive than buying the newest car or electronic gadget.

Notice how the exchanges below help create some space between the desire for the thing and the thing itself. The focus then shifts to the need that the thing is supposed to meet, and allows consideration of whether it will actually meet the need in the long term.

EXAMPLES:

Partner: "I need a car."
>You: "Would having the car give you freedom to move around?"
>—Or—
>You: "Do you want to have a car to be able to get to work on time?"
>—Or—
>You: "Would having the car give you more control?"

Partner: "I really can't lose this job right now!"
>You: "Is it that you want structure and predictability?"
>—Or—
>You: "Is it the structure and predictability, or being able to take care of your family?"

Partner: "I really need the extra money from my bonus this year."
>You: "Is that about security and stability?"
>—Or—
>You: "Would having the extra money give you some important peace of mind?

TECHNIQUE #11: DISCONNECTING NEEDS FROM TIME

Modern society is very time-conscious, and this can easily lead us to conflate needs with strategies about doing things in a particular time-frame. Maybe you know someone who gets very anxious about schedules or who is always saying, "We *have* to get there on time." Maybe you *are* that person.

Notice how the phrase "we have to..." functions as an absolute and leaves no space for other alternatives. Do you really "have to," or is it just that you don't like the consequences if you don't? If you switch out of "have to," how does that change your experience?

You don't have to live without options. By considering the needs you think will be met if you get there on time, or fulfill some other goal in the timeframe you want, you can open up the conversation. You can similarly support others to see more options by helping them find the needs they are trying to meet when they are fixated on time.

EXAMPLES:

Partner: "I have to be there on time."
You: "Is it important to you to be on time so you can keep your agreements?"
—Or—
You: "Is this about trust and reliability for you, about your integrity in how you hold agreements?"
—Or—
You: "Do you want to show care and consideration?"

Partner: "I needed to get this report done yesterday!"
You: "When you say that, do you want to meet your need for reliability?"
—Or—
You: "Are you keen to support your team by having this report available for the next set of decisions you have planned?"
—Or—
You: "Do you want to give a sense of trust and reliability?"

Partner: "I need my business to be successful now, not in a year!"
You: "Is that because you would like sustainability and to contribute in a meaningful way?"
—Or—
You: "Is that about wanting to have the companionship of others who have successful businesses?"

FOR FURTHER PRACTICE

After using the examples above as your starting point, use real situations where you are clear about your strategy, but are not sure about the needs that are motivating you. Ask your partner to support you in uncovering those needs by making guesses as to what those needs might be. You might want to refer to the list of needs in Appendix C as you practice. Remember that there's no such thing as a bad guess. In these exercises, guessing wrong is often as effective as guessing correctly, as it gives the other person a chance to inquire internally and identify a more accurate motivation.

As always, take some time at the end of your practice to de-brief each other about what helped you the most.

FINDING STRATEGIES TO MEET ALL THE NEEDS

As with observations and feelings, uncovering the need can create a fundamental shift inside you. When you uncover what is motivating you to feel or act a certain way, your physiology changes. Suddenly, you feel greater clarity within yourself and greater capacity to connect with others.

Once you realize that everything you do or say is a strategy to meet a need, you can check in with yourself at any time. Whether you are in a conversation or a conflict, or just going about your daily activities, you are doing something that meets some need. Refer to Appendix C, if you have to, so you can get in the habit of naming that need. By increasing your awareness in this way, you'll find you can quickly access your needs whenever you find yourself in a difficult situation. That's valuable in itself, to help your body relax. It also will let you choose to meet the need via a broader array of strategies, and you'll be able to choose the strategies that align with your values.

When asking someone else to understand what's going on with you, it's useful to clarify your need so that they can better connect with what you're going through. Take care not to link that person to your need, because this is confusing your need with a strategy. (It also will likely make it harder for the person to connect with you.)

Being able to make this separation between needs and people becomes even more critical in the kinds of ongoing conflicts that can happen with the people closest to us. It can be especially difficult to avoid seeing your well-being as reliant on your intimates doing something for you or being somewhere for you, and all by a particular time. But it only pours fuel on the fires of conflict when you express your desires in this way; the other person hears a demand and reacts.

When you notice that you have a strategy that is tied to a person, place, time, or thing, ask yourself why you want it. Let's say that you want your partner to clean up the table after dinner. What would having that happen do for you?

When you help yourself to unpack the needs tied up in a strategy, you may discover there are multiple layers of needs. If your partner cleaned up the table after dinner, that might provide the cleanliness you value. It might also help you feel equality about the sharing of work, since you're the one who makes the dinner every night. Going another layer deeper, you might realize that your partner cleaning up the dishes also meets a need for care. The needs for cleanliness, equality, and care can all be met by your partner cleaning off the table. However—and this is important—they could also be met in some other way. This confirms that you have successfully separated your needs from a person.

Once you get clear about needs you want to meet, you can begin to talk to your partner in a very different way. Instead of saying, "I need you to clear the table," you will be able to tie a specific request to the needs it would meet for you. For example, "Would you help me clear the table so I can sit down and relax? I haven't been able to do that all day."

Practice Pause

Plan how you will increase your awareness of the needs motivating your actions.

* * * * * *

At Maggie's request, Uncle Gerry and Aunt Peg were both on the sidelines of her Friday evening soccer match. Gerry and James stood off to one side, shouting encouragements to Maggie and her teammates. Once Sally had finished serving the half-time snack, she drew a deep breath and sought out Peg.

"Have an orange slice?"

"No, thanks. But I'm impressed at how you laid them out on trays like that. This is why you're the perfect mother, Sal. It's also why you drive the rest of us crazy."

"Heeey," Sally felt slightly wounded. "The trays aren't a big deal. They're just what I had around and it seemed like the most hygienic—". Sally broke off when she realized her sister was smiling at her, but with eyes that were wet with tears.

"I love being asked to come to Maggie's game," Peg said. "You have such great kids, and I'd really enjoy living this much closer to everyone again. This town used to be my home, too, you know. If I came back here, I'd not only save some money, I'd also be coming back to a place where I still have a lot of friends."

"And family," said Sally. "You always have us, Peg. You know you can always stay with us whenever you want."

Peg turned her face to look back at the soccer field. "I appreciate that. I really do. But I was talking to Mom and I think that her needs and my needs are the same. We love our families, but we also cherish our privacy and our *independence. We want to stay independent as much as we can."*

"There's nothing wrong with taking a little help..." Sally began. Then she stopped. "I want to help. But I'm realizing that my desire to help may be more connected to my own needs than to yours. I can hear you telling me that you have needs for shelter, peace of mind around money, and a sense of family and community. And both you and Mom value your autonomy."

Peg nodded vigorously. "That's right! That's exactly it. And I don't want to hurt your feelings, Sally. You are so, so good, and always so generous. You and James, both."

Sally shook her head. "I just love you guys and I want everybody to be happy." She grew quiet for a moment, then chuckled. "At this point, my friend Alicia would ask, 'So what is it about their being happy that would make you happy, Sally?'"

"And how would you answer?"

"If you and Mom are happy...and safe...then that would meet my needs for peace of mind. And for calm and rest. Oh, and I would really love you living in town again, Peg. That would meet my need for companionship. So much!"

Peg threw an arm around Sally and squeezed. "Are you really okay with this? Should we talk to Gerry about this? Maybe set up some agreements about how this could work? I know there are a lot of details to sort out around Mom's at-home recovery care. Maybe we could set up a trial period, to start."

"I like that idea," nodded Sally. "I think Gerry and Mom will like it, too."

The crowd roared its excitement as one of Maggie's teammates scored a goal. Sally and Peg looked at each other and grinned.

NEXT UP

Once we are in touch with what is motivating ourselves or another person, we are in a position to find a strategy that would satisfy us. In the next chapter, we will look at requests and how we can use them not only to meet our needs, but also to create connections with those around us.

6 | What Do You Want to Do?
Finding Requests

James remembered the sensation of his anger as having felt like a scorching liquid surging up through his torso and into the muscles of his throat. In his rage at seeing the report card and finding Corey at the house, he'd wanted to punish his son. He wanted to shame Corey for being a slacker and a sneak.

Touching his fingertips to his brow, James sank into a chair. Why was school suddenly a struggle for his son? Before this fall, Corey had never gotten lower than a B-. And he certainly would never have skipped out on a sports practice. What could be going on? And why was Corey acting so defensive and cavalier?

This was the hardest part of being a parent sometimes. The constant ache and worry over your kids' happiness. Well, starting tomorrow, he and Corey could just start getting up early in the mornings to do some extra study. James would force Corey to take more time on his homework until those grades came up again. Sure, it might be unpleasant in the short term, but someday Corey would thank him for it.

Suddenly, an image popped into James' head. It was the image of his own father pounding the table and bending down to holler in James' face. James' stomach lurched at the memory. He had dreaded the nights when his father had tried to help him with his homework. ("Come on, Jimmy! Just focus, for once, and get it done!") Eventually, James had learned never to show any self-doubt when his father was watching. He took pains to hide his mistakes, because these seemed to push his dad over the edge.

His father hadn't been a cruel man. Not a bit. But James shuddered to remember how it felt to see his father heat up and "lose it" whenever James had really disappointed him. It felt stressful and scary to be the cause of all that frustration—and it made James want to avoid his dad at all costs.

What if Corey was experiencing exactly the same stress and fright that I did with my father? James' felt his throat tighten at the thought. "This is not who I wanted to be," he whispered. "I have to do something about this pattern, or I'm just going to push Corey away. Are there specific requests I can make of Corey—and of myself—that would help turn things around?"

* * * * * *

Our culture often sends the message that it pays to be tough. It suggests that you can only get what you want if you are single-minded, firm and uncompromising. Tenacity can be a good thing, no doubt. But if you get what you want by using some form of coercion—be it force, or inducement of fear, guilt, shame or obligation—you will probably not like the consequences as much as if you use a process of collaboration.

Making a demand typically creates more resistance in the other person. Let's say a parent is trying to get her young child to take a bath. "It's time to put your toys away and get into the bathtub," she says. The child hears that statement as a demand, and says, "No! I don't want to! I took a bath yesterday. Why do I always have to take a bath? I hate taking baths!" The parent responds, "Why are you acting like this?

You know you have to take a bath," and the situation turns into a power struggle in which both parent and child get increasingly agitated. The parent might become so upset that she uses physical force to drag the child into the bath, or she may use threats to get the child into the bathtub. The struggle can turn into a horrible, or even traumatic, experience for them both.

What happens in the aftermath of the bath incident? Maybe there are harsh words and tears. Maybe the parent and child become shut off and disconnected from one another, using body language and icy looks to demonstrate their disdain for each other. The child, who perceives himself as having experienced an emotional hurt around being forced to do something he didn't want to do, may become sullen and withdrawn. When it's bath-time again, both parent and child will be primed for the exact same conflict, and a pattern takes form. The child may grow even more resistant. Or, if the child feels afraid of the parent's anger and retaliation, he may become resigned around bath time, and then will act out in other ways, perhaps by not cooperating at school or by dragging his feet when it's time to leave the house. Unconsciously or not, the child will show his hurt and anger by doing things that make life more difficult and frustrating for the parent.

The dynamics around the bath-time struggle are not unique to parenting. The same dynamics play out in any situation where there is demand energy. It doesn't matter if you are hearing a demand from your boss, from a friend, or from your spouse. A demand will almost certainly trigger your resistance. If you feel forced to do something, you may well do it, but your displeasure will show up somewhere.

Now picture yourself as the one who is trying to force someone else to do something. Probably you want compliance for a specific reason and you may feel pressure to get to agreement quickly. But the reality is that you ultimately cannot make others bend to your will. The tantrums generated by emotional overwhelm in a two-year-old child and the autonomy tantrums of teenagers of all ages prove this. You cannot make anybody do anything, however much you would like to. The only thing you can do is to create consequences that the other person doesn't like, or punish them physically or emotionally.

> Marshall Rosenberg makes this point by saying:
> *You can't make anybody do anything.*
> *You can only make them wish they had.*
> *And if you make them wish they had,*
> *They will make you wish you hadn't.*

Making effective requests instead of demands means using a collaborative approach in your communications. Using the six request techniques offered in this chapter will increase the odds that your requests will work. It also will reduce the chance that others will hear your requests as demands.

DEMANDS VS. REQUESTS

Early in Sally and James' relationship, Sally used to feel a lot of stress around hosting family gatherings at their home. By James' account, Sally would "freak out" at him before each event, saying, *"Why aren't the dishes put away? Why do I have to do everything? Your stuff is everywhere. I never get the support I need and you don't listen and don't care."* James would inevitably grow defensive and angry. Hearing Sally say those words didn't meet his need to be recognized for what he had done and to be seen for the ways in which he did show her that he cared. Eventually, it became James' habit to respond to Sally with reflexive counter-criticisms. He would accuse her of only remembering the bad things about their relationship and of addressing him more harshly than she would ever dream of talking to anyone else. By the time the first batch of extended family members turned up, neither Sally nor James would be in the mood to enjoy their company.

Each person in a conflict tends to see himself as a victim, and this feeds feelings of anger, upset, and hurt. If you ask for something from the other person when you are having these feelings, you'll likely *sound* as if you're making a demand (whether or not you intend to do so), and this will deepen the conflict instead of moving it toward a resolution. When Sally spoke to James in her moment of overwhelm, she was actually issuing a call for help. But it came out sounding like a demand, and this exacerbated the conflict with James.

Making clear, doable requests for what we want is not a skill that is taught or frequently modeled for us. (Neither is hearing the "please" in an upset person's demands.) Most people ask for what they want in ineffective ways that sometimes lead to exactly what they don't want. For example, they may ask for something in a way that is too vague or that is based on a negative ("Would you stop being so annoying?"). They may use language that implies they will only be satisfied with a "yes." Or they may be overly concerned about not appearing "bossy" or "controlling," and so they become too afraid to ask for what they want. Then they get upset with the people around them for not having guessed what it was they wanted.

Typically, a request will sound like a demand whenever you mix up your needs with your strategies. This happens when you feel certain that your need can only be met if the other person does what you say. If this inner tension exists, your language may technically suggest that the other person has a choice in how to respond to your request, but your voice and your demeanor will have a demand energy that will cause the other person to resist.

From the previous chapter, you know that there can be great value in moving from the specific to the general. (That's the best way to locate your underlying needs when all your brain and mouth can come up with are strategies.) In order to formulate a true request, however, it helps to let your thoughts flow in the opposite direction—from the *general to the specific.* Once you've named your need, you can work on formulating a request for some action that can get your need met.

In the techniques section below, we will describe these characteristics of a request in more detail and help you learn how to create requests that are more likely to lead to what you want. Fundamentally, making requests is about creating an agreement that all involved are more likely to keep because it meets everyone's needs.

REQUESTS TECHNIQUES

Take a minute to reflect on all you have absorbed so far from this book in terms of the 4 Components of Communication ("OFNR"). You have learned how to support others to identify their **Observations** (versus judgments), to feel and name their **Feelings** (versus faux feelings), and connect with their **Needs** (versus strategies). Now comes the moment when you can help others (and also yourself!) to focus on the "R" in "OFNR," or to figure out what **Request** to make in order to meet needs. This will mean formulating a *present-tense, positive* request that is phrased using *action language.* It will also mean supporting others (or yourself) in the intention to make a true request instead of a demand.

Below, we break out all the elements of an effective request into three techniques that you can practice. Each one of these techniques is important and, unlike the techniques in previous chapters, cannot succeed unless all three are used together. Together they are essential to reaching a strong agreement. You'll find you can make the kind of powerful requests that connect you with other people while also meeting your needs.

In each of the examples for the techniques below, you are helping someone else get clear in a specific way about what they want, and then we offer an example of how what they want would be turned into request language.

TECHNIQUE #12: MAKING PRESENT-TENSE REQUESTS

None of us can guarantee what we will do in the future. At most, you can agree now that you *intend* to do something at a later point. Perhaps a friend invites you to attend a Friday night movie. In agreeing to go, you are stating your present intention to meet your friend at a certain time and place at week's end. However, any number of situations could arise to prevent that from happening. Therefore, it helps to be clear, both in the agreements you make and in your requests of others, that the agreement is a present-tense intention regarding a future action. Even if you are asking someone to agree to plan to do something in the future, the act of agreement is done in the now.

In our Mediate Your Life trainings, we encourage our participants to keep their requests in the present tense. This may seem like hair-splitting, until you realize how often requests are expressed in the future tense. For example, you might ask, "Will you send me your report by 5 p.m. on Friday afternoon?" This is fine as long as you are clear in your mind that you are really asking, "Are you willing to agree *now* [from the vantage point of this present moment] to get the report in to me by Friday afternoon at 5 pm?" The attention to language and meaning can help you remember that requests are not "written in stone" on account of the unknowable future. This can save you a conflict down the road, because you can more easily remember to treat any variation from the original agreement as another opportunity to connect with the other person and yourself, instead of reacting with punishment and blame.

With your practice partner, use the examples to practice supporting your partner to formulate requests in the present tense. As always, make sure you switch roles so that both you and your partner get some experience in the supporting role. You can, of course, substitute personal examples in your practice, if you wish. Another way to practice this technique on your own is to notice throughout your day whether your requests are in present tense. If they are not, see if you can shift your thinking until you do regard them as present tense requests.

EXAMPLES:

Partner: "I really wish he would get home earlier!"
You: "What do you think you could do or say that would be more specific about what you want?"
Partner's example request: "Would you agree to be home by 6pm each day?"

Partner: "When my coworker gets upset and yells, I'd like to be less reactive."
You: "How can you imagine reminding yourself to do that the next time your coworker reacts like that?"
Partner's example agreement with herself: "Am I willing to remind myself each time I am meeting with this coworker that if he starts to get upset I will inhale three times before I respond in any way."
—OR—
You: "What do you think would help you actually be less reactive?"
Partner's example agreement with herself: "I agree to practice with my practice partner stopping and inhaling three times while she role-plays my coworker being upset."

Partner: "I'm tired of her being late to work. She should be here on time!"

You: "Do you want to have another conversation in which she confirms her understanding about arriving at work at the agreed-upon time?"

Partner's example request: "Co-worker, would you meet with me after the team meeting today to talk about your getting to work at the agreed-upon time?"

—OR—

You: "What do you imagine you could say to her that would result in her getting there when you would like?"

Partner's example request: "Would you help me understand what keeps you from getting to work when you have said you would?"

Partner: "I'm fed up with how he never calls me back after telling me that he will!"

You: "So do you want to reach an agreement with him about matching what he promises to do to what he actually does?"

Partner's example request: "Would you tell me if you would spend 10 minutes with me within the next week brainstorming ways I can be assured that when you say you will call me that you will?"

—OR—

You: "How do you think you can work with him so he's more likely to remember that he's said he will call you back?"

Partner's example request: "Is there something that I can do that would increase the likelihood that when you say you will return my call that you will return it?"

TECHNIQUE #13: MAKING POSITIVE REQUESTS

In this exercise, "positive" refers to requests being framed to say what the person wants as opposed to what they don't want.

Very often, you are moved to make a request because you notice someone doing something that you don't like. So it's not surprising that many requests get made in the negative; (E.g., "Could you quit leaving your dirty dishes all over the place?") There's nothing intrinsically problematic with stating what you don't want. But you're more likely to enjoy the results when you also verbalize what you *do* want.

A positive request is much easier for the other person to hear, because it sounds less like criticism and a demand. Which of these two sentences would you rather hear?

"Could you quit leaving your dirty dishes all over the place?" [Negative Request]

"Would you mind helping me to keep our apartment clean by putting your dishes in the sink after you are finished with them?" [Positive Request]

Saying what you don't want only tells the other person what you don't want, and leaves open to interpretation what you do want, making it less likely that you'll get it. Using a positive request makes what you do want perfectly clear.

With your practice partner, try shifting negative requests into positive requests. Use the examples below as a starting point. Then try formulating a real-life request regarding something that you don't like, and ask your partner's support in figuring out what you do want to have happen instead. (E.g., "I wish my upstairs neighbor would stop being so noisy late at night" could become, "I plan to ask my neighbor to talk to me about what it means to keep 'quiet hours' between 11 p.m. and 8 a.m.") After you both have a chance to practice, reflect together on what most helped you to make your request positive. Take this technique into your daily life by noticing when your requests are expressed in the negative and practice converting that request into a positive request.

EXAMPLES:

Partner: "I want him to stop leaving his clothes everywhere."
  You: "So you would like him to put away his clothes at the end of each day?"
  Partner's example request: "When you take your clothes off in our home, would you be willing to either put them in the dirty clothes hamper or hang them in your closet?"
  —OR—
  You: "Would you like him to put his dirty clothes in the hamper instead?"
  Partner's example request: "Would you keep the floor clear of your clothes, and either put them in the hamper or hang them in your closet?"

Partner: "She shouldn't be focusing so much on what is wrong all the time."
  You: "It sounds as if you would like her to focus on the positive?"
  Partner's example request: "Would you tell me two things that you like about your day?"
  —OR—
  You: "Would you like her to express what she is dissatisfied about in a way that is easier for you to hear?"
  Partner's example request: "When you tell me about something you are dissatisfied with, would it be okay with you to tell me the specific things that were said and done that you are displeased with?"

Partner: "He needs to stop being late to meetings all the time."
You: "Would you prefer that he be on time for meetings?"
Partner's example request: "Will you tell me what it would take for you to get to meetings at the planned start time?"
—OR—
You: "Would you like to work out some way that you can be assured he will arrive at the meetings when they start?"
Partner's example request: "What could I do, or someone else do, that might help you be with the rest of the team at the meeting start time?"
—OR—
You: "Do you want him to agree to be on time?"
Partner's example request: "Will you tell me when you plan to arrive for the next meeting?"

TECHNIQUE #14: MAKING REQUESTS IN ACTION LANGUAGE

A request is in "action language" if it is doable, concrete, and behavioral in the sense that it's an action that you can observe. It also will be obvious to everyone involved whether or not the request has been fulfilled. When one spouse says to another, "I want you to show me you love me!" that is not an action language request. To make the request doable and specific, the first spouse might instead say, "Would you be willing to have a cup of coffee with me in the morning before we both go to work?" That is in action language, because, unlike the "show-me-you-love-me" request, it has measurable or observable results. Either the shared coffee will happen, or it won't.

Once you start thinking in terms of action language requests, you will find others understand you better and can more accurately respond to your wishes. Below are some examples of vague requests turned into actionable requests. Which would you rather hear? And which will you use in the future?

Not Action Language	Action Language
"Would you please control yourself?"	"Would you speak to me with the same volume that I'm using to speak to you?"
"I'd like you to be more considerate."	"Please hold the door open for me when I'm carrying groceries."
"Could you please show me some appreciation?	"Could you tell me two things that I've done this week that you have liked?"

Notice how the phrases on the left stay at such a general level that it would be nearly impossible to figure out when and how the request has been met. The left-hand phrases also sound like criticisms, which could undermine your connection with the other person. That is why it's so important to make your request as specific as possible, identifying exactly what you hope will meet your needs. If it happens that you're on the receiving end of a vague request that does not seem concrete or doable, you can help the person making the request by guessing what a specific request might be, or simply ask for more information.

Use the examples below to guide you in your paired practice, and try out your own real-life examples if you can. You can also practice this technique throughout your day, by checking that your requests, and other people's requests to you, are stated in action language.

EXAMPLES:

Partner: "I wish he would show me that he loves me."

You: "What might he do that would meet your need for love?"

Partner's example request: "When you come home would you sit with me on the couch and tell me about your day?"

—OR—

You: "How would you like him to show you that he loves you?"

Partner's example request: "Each time you leave for work in the morning, would you kiss me goodbye and give me a hug?"

Partner: "She shouldn't be focusing so much on what is wrong all the time."

You: "Would you like her to acknowledge one thing that went well during the day?"

Partner's example request: "Would you tell me at least one thing that you liked about your day?"

—OR—

You: "Would you like her to talk about what went well during the day before talking about what didn't?"

Partner's example request: "Would you be willing to tell me one thing that went well for you today, before you tell about what you did not like?"

Partner: "I'd like them to appreciate all that I do at work."

You: "So is that about getting a raise, or is it more that you would like to be recognized for what you have accomplished?"

Partner's example request: "Would you raise my pay by seven percent, starting this next pay period?"

—OR—

You: "Would appreciation in this case mean being told regularly what you are doing that is making a valuable contribution?"

Partner's example request to a work colleague: "Do you like my contribution to the project we just completed?"

MAKING REQUESTS OF YOURSELF

If you can formulate present-tense, positive requests that are expressed in action language, you're going to like the results—even and especially when the request is directed at yourself! Personal integrity begins with keeping your agreements with yourself, but this is difficult when you make requests of yourself that are vague, unrealistic, or steeped in self-criticism.

For example, if James said to himself, "I want to stop 'losing it' like my father every time Corey drives me up a wall," he is setting himself up for failure and will likely end up feeling bad about himself. Imagine if he put his intention in the form of a positive request, "I would like to stay calm and speak at a normal volume whenever I feel angry or afraid about something that Corey does."

Ideally, James would make an agreement with himself that allowed him to re-commit to his goal after any "lapse" and that included frequent check-ins and supports. For example, James could take a series of concrete actions, such as:

- "For the next week I will keep a journal of my interactions with the kids and, after seven days, I will look at how I can improve my patterns with them both."
- "I am going to write in a gratitude journal—with each entry written as a note to Corey—for at least 15 minutes each day this week."
- "I am going to enlist Sally for daily check-ins and self-connection practice."

- "I will celebrate my incremental successes by doing something I enjoy, such as going for a long bike ride or taking the family out for pizza."

Each of the above is present tense, positive, and in action language. Whether or not James would create a list exactly like this one, it would probably be an enormous relief to see his intention "chunked" into such simple and doable tasks, all designed to support him in what could be a bumpy transition. James could easily check to see whether he had fulfilled each request, and if not, he and his check-in partner, Sally, could consider what needs he was meeting instead.

Whether making a request of yourself or someone else, ask yourself the following questions about your request:

- "Am I asking for a future action? If so, can I be clear that I am requesting it as a present intention?" (Checks that it is present tense.)
- "Am I asking for what I want? If not, how can I shift this request to ask for what I want versus what I don't want?" (Checks that it is positive.)
- "How will I know that this request has been fulfilled?" (Checks that the request is in action language.)

* * * * * *

James thought back on his feelings and needs to see if any requests might come to the surface. He reflected on his needs for respect, cooperation, and understanding what was going on for Corey. He realized he also wanted to feel some hope regarding his son's situation and some reassurance that his son was going to be okay.

"A first step might be to ask Corey what has been going on for him at school lately. That would help me understand him better. I would also like to understand why he chose to be absent from practice this afternoon." James paused to

reflect and concluded that wanting to understand these two things is crucial for him right now.

"If I understand better what was going on for him, I might be able to help him, by asking him to shift in some way. What could I ask him that I think would give me hope and reassurance? Well, I want him to stop avoiding his problems and to quit the defiant, sneaky teen routine!" James smiled despite himself, recognizing that his request was not at all doable and expressed what he didn't want instead of what he did want. Still, he could see this might be a good place to start.

"What do I actually want Corey to do? Well, I want him to not wait until his grades are in the toilet before he asks for help. So...I would like him to talk to Sally and me before things hit a crisis point. I know that is what I would like, though I'll have to see whether that still makes sense for him based on whatever has been going on for him today."

James worried a bit more about replicating some of the less helpful habits of his father, and not being able to connect with his son. He wanted to be respected, yes, but that was really about wanting to be seen by Corey and to contribute to Corey's well-being.

"I'm having trouble coming up with a specific request that captures all of this, so I'll check in with Sally to see if I can set up an agreement with her about how I respond to the things that Corey does that I feel frustrated about. In the meantime, my request to myself is that I take three deep breaths the minute I realize that I am starting to get angry about something Corey is doing. Three deep breaths before I respond to him in an even tone. I'll do the breaths no matter what Corey might say, and I'll do them even if he gives me the silent treatment. I'd like to go to bed tonight knowing that I stayed in a cool-headed, non-yelling frame of mind until I can check in with Sally tonight."

With his requests and next steps clear, James feels complete for the moment and ready to move on with the rest of the evening.

> **Practice Pause**
> Think of a recent request you made of yourself or another person. Was it a present-tense, positive request, expressed in action language? If not, how could you have made it so?

TECHNIQUE #15: CONFIRMING THE MESSAGE WAS RECEIVED

At times, you will want to know whether the message you sent is the same message that the other person received. A common communication pitfall is to assume that you understand or have been understood, without checking to make sure that is the case. That so many conflicts arise from this problem is sad, because it is so simple to ask whether you and the other person are actually on the same page.

If a conversation has been focused on what's going on for you, the request is, "Would you be willing to tell me what you heard me say?" The other person responds with what she heard (or with her interpretation of what she heard), which gives you a chance to clarify if she has not heard you the way you would like.

If you've been focused on the other person's experience, you can make a similar request to ensure that you have heard that person the way she would like to be heard. You might say, "Are you willing to pause for me to make sure I'm hearing you the way you want me to?" If she says yes, then reflect back, in your own words or in her words, what you understand she is trying to communicate. She can then correct or expand on what you have said to get her point across more clearly.

You can practice this technique in your daily life whenever people ask, "Do you understand what I'm telling you?" or some variation of that question. The expected response is either "yes" or "no," but neither of these answers is very satisfying. Saying, "Yes, I understand" doesn't tell the person *what* you understood, which may, in fact, be very different from what that person wanted you to understand. If the speaker wants to make sure his message is received, respond with something like, "Well, let me make sure I understand. This is what I heard you saying….[Summary of what you heard]. Is that right?" If you want to make sure someone else understands you, simply ask this way: "Would you be willing to tell me what you heard me say?"

TECHNIQUE #16: TESTING THE QUALITY OF YOUR CONNECTION

Besides making sure that you have been heard the way you would like, you also might want to check the quality of your connection with the other person. By using feelings, you can take a measurement, so to speak, of how connected the other person is with you and with what you are saying. Feelings provide a rich shorthand: pleasurable feelings generally indicate connection; unpleasant or painful ones indicate that connection may be lacking.

For the most part, you will make a request that tests the quality of your connection when you have been focused on your own experience. When you've shared something, you can simply append this request to the end of your last sentence: "How do you feel hearing what I just said?"

You can also rephrase this request so it contains no reference to feeling. For example, "How is it for you that…" or "What's your reaction to…?" or even, "What do you think about what I've said?" These options offer another way to assess how well you've been heard. How other people respond will give you clues both about what they heard you say and to how they are reacting to it.

You can also let the other person know how connected you are to what he has been saying. You might say, "I'm feeling skeptical when I hear that…" or "I feel happy hearing you say that…." If prompted, you can add a few more details about why, and then you can ask the other person how he feels having heard what you just said. In other words, the quality-of-connection requests can keep flowing back and forth.

Testing the quality of connection can be applied either to the conversation in general or to a specific idea that you have just floated. For example, you might ask, "How do you feel about my idea of asking your dad for a loan to fix the roof?" Assessing the quality of connection to an idea can help to gauge the ongoing connection between you and another person, which can suffer if you repeatedly find yourself out of sync regarding the ideas of actions you will take together.

Notice how the quality-of-connection request is much like the confirming-the-message request. Both fit the basic criteria of an effective request (present-tense, positive, expressed in action language). You are asking someone in the present moment what she heard or how she feels about it. You are asking for what she wants instead of what she doesn't want. Both connection requests are also expressed in action language—they are specific and doable, and you can reasonably know whether they have been fulfilled or not.

TECHNIQUE #17: MAKING SOLUTION REQUESTS

Solution requests ask for actions that will meet your needs. This kind of request is about what you would like to have happen in the world, and you can make it either of yourself or of other people. What you are asking is for something that will contribute to your well-being. Here are some examples of solution requests:

- Would you mind passing the eggrolls?
- How about if I move in with Mom and help care for her?
- Would you be willing to tell me why you put on your headphones?
- Would it help if I attended the parent-teacher meeting with you?
- How about we have our meeting next Monday, at 3pm, here in our offices?

You might have noticed that, in all of the techniques outlined in this book, you've been practicing making requests with your partner. When you support someone else to get clear about her observation, feelings, needs, and requests, you are essentially making one request after another. As you continue to practice the techniques with a partner, add into your debrief time a discussion about any ways that your requests might be more connecting. Ask your partner how she felt when you phrased requests one way versus another. The more experience you have in making requests and getting feedback about what felt connecting to another person and what did not, the better you will be able to connect with someone through your requests.

Keep track in some way of your experience, perhaps by keeping a journal of particularly effective requests that you make of others and others make of you. As you practice, remember that the point isn't to "get it right." It's about making hundreds of practice requests, so you have many examples to draw from and learn from.

Practice Pause

What's the most connecting request that someone has made of you lately? What did you like about the way the request was posed to you? How do you think you would have responded if the request had been expressed differently?

---

* * * * * *

James and Sally were curled up together on the couch, feeling surprise that the day's events had gone so well.

"I can't believe that you and Gerry and Peg came to an agreement."

"I know! I'm feeling really hopeful about this, especially since Ger agreed to the trial period." Sally smiled at her husband. *"I also can't believe how great you were with Corey's guidance counselor today. I really appreciate you upending your schedule so you could make that appointment."*

"It was either that or continue to scream and yell at the kid," sighed James. *"And that's exactly what I don't want to do anymore."* James told Sally about his fear that he was treating Corey the way his own father had treated him.

Sally sat very still as she absorbed James' words. *"It sounds like it's really important for you to treat Corey in a different way."*

James sat up. *"Yes. I'm just so scared that we'll lose him. It's also painful for me to think about how it was for me when my dad would say and do those things. Corey is in high school now. I remember when I got into high school I started rebelling big time. I don't want to push him away even more."*

"So, how would you like to interact with him?"

James paused for a moment. *"I just want to enjoy being with him. He's probably not going to be living under our roof for much longer, you know. That's why it feels so awful when I get so angry that I just explode at him. If I'm honest, I want to frighten him into doing what I want, and that's just pushing him away. So, instead of reacting, I want to stay curious about what's going on with him. You know, that's really what I wanted anyway, to know what's happening that suddenly caused his grades to dip. So, yeah, I'd like to connect with him from a space of curiosity and enjoyment."*

Sally nodded. *"I like that. I can see how you might have been curious, but instead of coming from there you were caught up in the fear of losing him and reacted out of that. What could help you to remember this next time?"*

"I think it would help to be able to keep my intention in mind whenever I'm going to interact with him." James tapped his temple with one finger. *"That way it might become more ingrained, and I might actually remember it the next time I get really angry. Maybe I can put a note up somewhere to remind me."*

"What if we put the word "curiosity" on the bathroom mirror? That way I'll see it, too. I'd love it if I could always relate to both Corey and Maggie from joy and curiosity."

Sally looked down at her lap for a moment, then back up at James. "You know, I notice when you start to go there with Corey, and I'm wondering— is there any other way I can support you more directly? How about if I hear you raising your voice, or doing something that I interpret as not coming from joy and curiosity, I'll let you know. What could I do that would support you in that moment?"

James furrowed his brow. "I don't know. If I'm already going down the road, it's already too late. But maybe not.... Maybe if you interrupt me and ask me something.... How about if you say, 'Who are you right now?' That might jolt me into seeing that I'm acting like my dad used to."

"Okay, let's try it!" Sally took James' hand and squeezed it. "Next time I notice you reacting in that way I will ask you, 'Who are you right now?' Just promise you won't shoot the messenger, okay?"

James laughed. "I'll do my best."

AWARENESS THROUGH AGREEMENTS

James made an agreement with Sally to help him come more quickly to a state of awareness when he started to react in ways that he didn't like. Why couldn't he just figure this out on his own? Couldn't he just resolve to be more aware of his own tendencies, so he could choose to ignore them?

If only it were that simple. Awareness is a slippery thing. Consider the language of awareness and how it suggests that humans have precious little to do with our own process of becoming aware:

"I just woke up…"

"The insight hit me…"

"The light bulb went off, and I realized…"

"I got this epiphany…."

You either are aware, or you are not, and you can easily drift in and out of awareness. Awareness is sometimes said to "arise." And if you experience something like a "growing" awareness, it is probably because "aha!" moments of awareness are coming more frequently and staying for longer. But awareness makes no promises. You can be aware now *of how you have not been aware in the past, but you cannot guarantee* to yourself or anyone else (despite your best intentions to be so!) that you're still going to be aware at any point in the future.

Awareness is noticing—but in a very particular way. In a moment of awareness, or in those moments when you "wake up," you may enjoy a sense of double perception. That is, you find you can use your senses to notice what is outside of you, at the same time that you are able to monitor your internal states—physiological, mental, and emotional.

The Mediate Your Life approach is designed to help you gain the kind of awareness that links to self-knowledge. For instance, you might engage a friend in a conversation that seemed superficial and light, but that leaves you feeling uneasy. Later, you realize that you missed an important cue and didn't respond to the friend as you would have liked. That is an after-the-fact awareness, but it's still quite useful. It gives you the information to adjust your responses going forward.

In our trainings, we often speak about the difficulty of "getting off the toboggan" when you're so flooded with intense emotions that it can feel impossible to slow the momentum of your descent down a destructive, angry, or even violent path.

James had to plunge all the way to the bottom of the toboggan hill with Corey before he was able to self-connect and regain awareness—in his case, an awareness that he was replicating a conflict habit that had been modeled for him by his father.

What if James had managed to regain that awareness at the top of the slope, before his toboggan had gone shooting downhill? His conversation with Corey would have turned out quite differently.

But again, there is no "first step" to awareness. That's because awareness—and especially awareness in response to conflict—isn't something you can "do." Luckily, noticing that you are triggered into a reaction *is* a capacity you can develop through practice and repetition (we promise!) and this practice will bring with it an uncanny awareness of what is going on inside you.

As part of your practice, it's useful to enlist others' support to help you regain awareness and avoid destructive conflict habits. Make an agreement that supports you in being the person you want to be. Frame your agreements—and the reminder that you're requesting—in terms of what you want to create, not what you want to avoid.

James and Sally made a highly specific agreement about the exact words Sally would say to James whenever he got triggered into his old conflict habits. Do the same with your support person about exactly what he can do or say to support you. This will lessen the chances that you will react badly in the moment he says it. The "awareness password" can then succeed as a prompt to pull you back to your specific intention.

Practice Pause

Who can you make an agreement with to support your awareness of a habit that you would like to change?

In the following story, the last in this book from our family, you will read how James' agreement with Sally and intention to act differently with Corey plays out in their next interaction. This dialogue references many of the skills and techniques that have been discussed in this and earlier chapters. For more on integrating the four components and the techniques into conversation, also see Appendix D, "Putting It All Together."

* * * * * *

Corey yanked the plastic liner from the trashcan without noticing that it had snagged on the hinge of the trashcan lid. Swinging the plastic sack to his shoulder, he was halfway to the garage before his mother sounded the alarm. "Corey! The bag! Trash is going everywhere!"

A minute later, Corey was on his hands and knees, grumpily wiping up the smelly, sticky mess that he had accidentally strewn across the kitchen floor.

"Hey, Cor. I didn't see you there." James had strolled into the kitchen and was trying to act casual. "So, what homework do you have for tonight?"

Corey muttered something that James couldn't hear, so he repeated the question.

This time, Corey scooped up a wad of coffee grounds and flung them into the sink. "Haven't you people ever heard of composting?"

James raised an eyebrow. "Don't take that tone. I asked you a simple question."

Corey looked ready to explode. "I told you, I already did it. I don't need you watching over me every second."

James snorted. "Based on your grades, it seems like you do!"

Sally called out gently to James, her voice low and even as she asked their agreed-upon question: "Who are you right now?"

James exhaled sharply and felt himself coming back to awareness. As he'd practiced, he immediately drew a deep breath, then another one, making sure to extend the out-breath. He suddenly felt the tension that was gripping his entire body. He noticed how his heart was racing in his chest. After giving himself a moment to explore these sensations, he found himself focused on a tightness in his stomach and on the image of an erupting volcano trapped within a hollow iron ball. Struggling to name whatever he was feeling, he first came up with "anger," before recognizing that, beneath that anger, there was dread and desperation.

By naming his feelings, James felt some of the tension lift. For a split second, there was insight. He remembered that he wanted connection with his son more than he wanted to be right. He also remembered that his anger with Corey was so strong because, when James was young, he hadn't gotten the connection he wanted with his own father, and his current reactions were being driven by that old pattern.

With these thoughts, James felt calmer, lighter, and in touch with what was really going on for him. He began to wonder why Corey had reacted the way he had to James' inquiry.

James had a fleeting urge to share how his relationship with Corey's grandfather was driving his own anger, but thought better of it, worrying that too much "relationship stuff" would just push Corey away.

So James made a conscious decision to focus on Corey and what he might be going through. He started with a guess, one based on his own recollections of being a teenager.

"Corey..."

Corey climbed to his feet. "What?"

James hid his surprise as he noticed that Corey was now almost as tall as he. (And the kid wasn't even wearing shoes!) "I guess you would really like to know that your *mom and I trust you, huh?"*

Corey rolled his eyes. "Hello? I'm not a kid anymore."

Although James felt a twinge of irritation at Corey's tone and his choice of words, James continued focusing on his breath and his desire to connect with his son. He decided to say nothing, so Corey could say the things he wanted to say.

After an awkward pause, James' patience was rewarded. Corey continued, "I wish you guys could lay off a bit. I mean, what do you guys really remember about high school anymore? Why won't you cut me any slack?"

James remembered to take another deep breath and just to be present with Corey. He worked hard to do nothing other than let Corey's words soak into him, without James trying to puzzle out what they might mean. He listened "into the space between Corey's words," as Sally's Mediate Your Life training had taught them both to do.

James moved from being present to being ready to offer silent empathy, and to wonder again to himself where Corey was coming from and what he really wanted. In his mind, James thought, "I wonder if Corey is interpreting what I say to mean I'm trying to control him, instead of that I care about him." James guessed that Corey felt disgruntled and maybe hurt because he wanted to be seen as responsible and capable.

James reflected back what he understood Corey to be saying; "Yeah, you're not a kid anymore. You want to be treated like a fifteen-year-old and you want your mother and me to acknowledge that there are things about your high school experience that we don't understand."

"Sure, that'd be a nice change," said Corey, with audible sarcasm.

James knew from Corey's response that Corey still did not trust that he was being heard, so James continued to try to connect with his son by extending empathy. "It sounds like you experience the way we treat you as if we're using an old computer program. You're telling me that an upgrade is needed to match current reality."

(James hoped this language might resonate with Corey, who had a weak spot for all things computers.)

"'Upgrade.' Yeah, but I hope you're not trying to say something rude about my midterm report card right now..."

James laughed despite himself. "No! No, I'm not. Really. I'm just trying to figure out what are the underlying needs here. It sounds as if you would really like to be treated with respect for your ability to be responsible and to manage your own life, is that right?"

Corey's shoulders dropped a bit as he replied, "Yeah. Yeah, Dad, I got this. I'm on top of it, so stop laying into me about everything."

James felt a mild flash of irritation over how a question about homework had turned into "laying into [Corey] about everything." But he held back this thought, choosing instead to stay curious about Corey's perspective, "So, you're asking for some freedom and space around your school work?"

For the first time since they had begun talking, Corey looked straight at his father. "Exactly," he said, nodding.

James hoped that Corey's affirmative answers were evidence that he now felt heard. He decided to test whether Corey has been heard enough and was now able to hear his father's perspective.

"I can understand how frustrating it can be to want that kind of freedom, and I hear how you want us to trust you to make your own decisions. I'd also like to make that upgrade. What would help me is to know that you understand the consequences of decisions you make. Would you be willing to tell me what you just heard me say?"

Corey answered quickly, and without sarcasm this time. "You want to know that I've thought things through. And I have, I know it wouldn't be good to keep my grades where they are. Mr. Loewen and I made a plan."

Hearing this, James felt a release in his body. All four of his limbs—and even his lungs—suddenly felt more relaxed. He was almost giddy knowing that he and Corey had begun to hear each other.

James still wanted to be able to ask Corey about how things were going with grades and school, so he said, "Even as I make this 'upgrade'—no pun intended—I'm still going to want to know what's happening and to be able to ask you about school. I'm wondering how I could do that in a way that would work for you. Do you have any ideas?"

Corey frowned. "I don't want to be asked at all."

"Is that about privacy…?" James tried to uncover what had prompted Corey to say that.

Corey said, "No! I just… Look, if you ask, then that means you don't trust me."

James felt still more relief at hearing Corey's answer, because it helped him know what was going on. "Oh, okay, so it's not privacy. It's more that it's important to you that you have respect for your autonomy and trust for your decisions, is that it?"

"Yeah, I guess so." Corey shrugged.

"Okay. It wouldn't work for me not to ever ask you anything, because I love you, and part of loving you is wanting to be connected to what's going on for you. That's where I would like my questions to come from, not from a place of not trusting you. How about we agree that if I ask something and you think I might be coming from not trusting you, then you will ask me about it?"

Corey considered this for a moment, then asked, "Like, I could say, 'Why do you want to know?'"

James suspected he would be triggered if Corey asked that question with any attitude other than curiosity. But he decided it was important that Corey get to frame the question. "Sure, let's try that. And if I see you making a decision and want to know that you've thought it through, can I just ask you, 'Have you figured out the consequences?'"

"Yeah, okay."

Later that evening, James and Sally reflected on James' conversation with Corey. Sally was ecstatic that father and son had done so well with their communication. James still felt as if there was a lot of work for him to do. "I feel a lot of sadness knowing that he might be feeling alone in navigating high school. He basically was saying that our high school days are too far behind us for us to understand. So, there's a gap there...and we still don't really know what's going on for him at school. But at least I do feel like there was a little bit of opening there tonight. I feel some hope that I can keep trying to demonstrate to Corey how what I'm saying is coming from care and a desire to support him, not out of some judgment that he isn't capable of running his own life."

NEXT UP

Now that you have the tools and techniques to integrate Observations, Feelings, Needs, and Requests into your everyday conversation, we will wrap up with a few reminders about intention and practice, plus let you know what's coming up in the rest of the Mediate Your Life series.

Conclusion

"Reality is that which, when you stop
believing in it, doesn't go away."
— Philip K. Dick

Congratulations! By reading and practicing what is in this book, you've taken an important step to living the life you want to live.

Though this book is the foundation for the rest of the Mediate Your Life series, practicing and utilizing the skills you have learned here will enable you to be the author of your life. Using the four components of Observations, Feelings, Needs, and Requests helps you to create space between what happens and your reaction to it, a space where you can choose. As Victor Frankl said in the quote that began Chapter 2, "Between stimulus and response there is a space. In that space is our power to choose our response. In our response lies our growth and our freedom." In this book we've given you tools to be able to operate in this "Frankl space" where you are able to choose how you want to react and act. We hope that as you utilize these tools and practice in your daily life, especially in those challenging moments when you are stimulated into the fight/flight response, you will increasingly be able to choose peace.

Our intention is that integrating this material into your life will result in concrete, discernable changes. If you have been working actively with the material in this book, we encourage you to take some time to notice the changes you are experiencing. Celebrate what you have accomplished with your practice partner. The more you can notice and celebrate even the smallest steps you take and the tiniest improvements in your ability to react differently in difficult situations, the more you solidify a foundation for continued growth and change. Remembering that you have a choice when you get triggered and react habitually is a step. So is choosing not to react and taking a time out when normally you would escalate the situation and wage war instead of peace. These steps may not quite yet be where you would like to be, but in taking these steps and celebrating them you are moving that much closer to your goal.

If you read through the book and have not yet begun to practice and integrate the skills and way of thinking into your life, then congratulations for reading it. If you can see even a small hope for yourself, if after reading these pages you would like to be more in the driver's seat of your life, we encourage you to now begin to go back through and practice. Use the practice pauses to explore the concepts at a deeper level and find someone with whom you can practice the techniques. If you don't know anyone to practice with, connect with us through our website at http://www.mediateyourlife.com/ choosingpeace. This page has book extras, including a complete list of the techniques presented in this book, and resources for practicing with people in your life or creating a practice group. Also, if you come to one of our trainings, either in person or online, you will meet practice partners.

Besides a practice partner, you might also seek an accountability buddy, someone to check in with on a regular basis—daily or weekly—and share your commitments about practice and how you want to be in the world. We cannot overestimate the power of having somebody to tell what you're going to do and then check in on the next call about whether you did it. It's not only a tremendous support, as most of us find it incredibly difficult to be accountable to ourselves, it's also a practice in shifting out of blame and shame. You won't always have done all the things you said you would, and neither will your buddy. You can turn the times you haven't into practice moments, learning a new way to respond to commitments and promises that are not kept, even when you are the one who didn't keep them. Use Observations, Feelings, Needs, and Requests to reconnect with yourself and to support your partner when either of you have not fulfilled your agreements. With either a practice partner or accountability buddy, you can use everything that comes up between you as an opportunity for more practice, increasing your skills and capacity to work through conflict and disconnection.

We also want to welcome you; just in reading this book, and then by doing the practices and integrating these skills into your life, you are part of a larger community. This worldwide community is comprised of people like you—people who are seeking to be the authors of their own lives, to have more power to choose the way they would like to act, and to be able to live their highest intentions and values in the way they treat themselves and other people. While the work is our own, we can do that individual work best when we support each other. Whether you connect with this community personally or not, you are still a part of it. If you would like to have companionship in your process of change, please use the resources available on our website to find your place in this community.

Let's all work together to create the kind of world we would like for each other and for our children.

What's Next: The Mediate Your Life Series

The focus in this book has been for you to learn and practice the distinctions of Observation, Feelings, Needs, and Requests. Everything in later books will build on the foundation you have been creating as you work with the material in this book.

Each book in the rest of our series will focus on the tools, maps, and skills that we find useful to navigate conflict in different contexts or situations, such as the following:

- you are in conflict with a co-worker;
- you feel hurt when a friend tells you she cannot support you with a present difficulty;
- two of your siblings get into an argument;
- you find yourself unable to make a decision about something in your life;
- you feel anxious about an upcoming conversation;
- you feel bad about something that you did yesterday;
- a family member is hurt that you did not come to her party;
- your team at work is having trouble coming to a decision on how to proceed on a project.

The commonality underpinning all the different contexts of life that we will cover in later books in this series is that they are situations in which we get stimulated into some version of the stress response we talked about in depth in Chapter 1. The language components you learned in this book are the 25,000-foot view of what to do in these situations. In the maps we'll share in upcoming books we bring the view closer to the ground, giving you more specific steps of what to do to successfully bring yourself back to the present moment and make new choices in the situation. The more you practice and embody the basics of the distinctions you learned in this book, the easier it will be to integrate the maps and skills in the rest of the series. The rest of the books are essentially created out of the material in this book.

Having maps for specific conflict situations helps you with a structured way to remember to use the skills and tools you have when you are potentially triggered. Each map is a specific set of steps that helps you navigate the often confusing territory of conflict. This structure also allows you to consciously shift out of the paradigm of avoidance, punishment, blame, shame, and guilt, and into an active and accelerated plan for consciously creating what you want. You begin to change your behavior—to learn—in constructive ways that lead you toward living the life you choose.

The books in the rest of the series build upon each other in a particular way; it is helpful to learn certain maps before others, just as it's helpful to get the building blocks of this book before moving ahead. The flow through the books is not exactly linear; however, especially with the earlier books, we do recommend you read each one in order. The following description and flowchart will help you understand what is coming.

Books 2 and 3 both follow from this first book. Book 2 goes more in depth on interpersonal conflict, those times when you are in conflict with someone else, or are not yet in conflict but find conversations difficult with that person. The centerpiece of book 2 will be the Interpersonal Mediation map. Since it's important to know what to do leading up to a difficult conversation, as well as what to do afterwards, we share various processes that lead you through exactly how to handle a difficult conversation from the moment you know you will be in one through the process and the aftermath.

In book 3 we will take you through the maps that relate to conflict as an internal process. Most importantly, this book outlines how to work with all types of internal conflict, such as when you would like to do two things (but can't do them both), or when you would like to do something but know you shouldn't. Internal conflict also happens when something has already happened and you judge yourself for it; we will also help you work with those conflicts. This book is key to being more at peace with ourselves and to being able to take action consciously and in full alignment with what we would like to create.

Books 2 and 3 are both necessary to understand the full scope of book 4, which is about lending your skills to mediate between other people. Even if you think you don't ever need this skill, we recommend you read this book for a couple of reasons. First, conflict is all around us, and the more we have the skills to be able to help others through it, whether they are our kids, family members, or work colleagues, the better off everyone will be. Second, it helps to at least be familiar with the maps in book 4 to be able to understand the maps in the final three books.

Book 4 will focus on how to work with others when you are not directly involved in the conflict, using the tools of both mediation and conflict coaching. We'll share the five-step mediation model that serves as the primary map when you are mediating between others, whether you've been asked to mediate or are stepping in to support others in conflict without having been asked. We will explain the nine skills of mediation, and cover important mediation topics such as making solid agreements. In this book, we also cover conflict coaching, discussing how to work one-on-one with someone who is in conflict to support them to decide on and take the next step.

The topic of book 5 is conflict in community. How, as a leader in a community, can you more effectively resolve conflict? Whether you are a leader of your team at work or in your community, or are a parent, the maps and skills included in this book will help you navigate situations where you are supporting a group to make a decision. The maps we have developed for groups are included in this book, including the Group Decision Making Process and Group Mediation. These maps use some of the basic structure of mediation introduced in previous books and apply it to a setting where there are more than two parties in a conflict. Even if you are not in an official leadership role, we all can act as leaders by applying these skills.

In book 6 we talk about forgiveness. We have repeatedly found in our own personal lives and in our work with others that using the mediation skills we teach is about more than simply resolving conflict; it can result in healing our relationships and our past. We outline the Healing and Reconciliation Process and discuss the various ways to use it. This process is especially powerful in situations where one party feels hurt by another's actions, and can lead to forgiveness even if the person who was the "perpetrator" is not present. In situations where you are aware that your conduct resulted in someone else feeling hurt, a variation on this map can help you make amends and heal the rift in the relationship.

The final book in the series will help you integrate all of the maps presented in the series, seeing how they are all an integrated "map of maps" that you can use to navigate conflict in any context. Practice is a critical component to being able to integrate these skills into your life, and while how to practice will be covered in each book, in this final book of the series we will cover the variety of ways to practice moving forward. We discuss the power of role-playing and setting up your own practice mediations using real-life situations to both practice the skills and increase your capacity to use those skills. Since learning is the key result from practice, we present a model of a learning cycle that supports you in understanding the process you are going through. It is through practicing with our real-life situations that we learn and increase our capacity to use our skills when we are called to in the midst of a difficult situation.

Taken together, the seven books of the series represent our complete model of mediating your life, giving you the ability to successfully navigate conflict through responding moment-by-moment in a way that is in alignment with you and what you want to create in the world.

Epilogue
Following the Energy
by John Kinyon

"Take your time to understand.
Don't just do something, be there."
—*Marshall Rosenberg*

I want to share something with you that may at first sound shocking. Although Ike Lasater and I have spent more than a decade meticulously developing the Mediate Your Life approach, my hope is that you eventually won't need to remember and consciously apply what is in this book.

Sounds crazy, right? Let me explain: I want the distinctions and skills we've outlined in the preceding chapters to become so much a part of you that they are as natural and automatic as breathing.

I hope you one day find that you no longer need to think about what to do or say next in order to create a deeper connection with yourself and those around you.

Like my teacher, Marshall Rosenberg, I believe that the future of our shared planet hangs on our ability to turn conflicts into opportunities for growth and connection.

Without Marshall Rosenberg, there wouldn't be a Mediate Your Life training program. So much of what Ike and I teach together builds on Marshall's four decades of work as the founder of Nonviolent Communication, or NVC. Much of how I conceive of my work today is directly inspired by Marshall's example in the years I was able to study at his side. That's why I would like to conclude this volume by sharing with you what

Marshall taught me about the NVC skills and distinctions and the source of their power. I will tell you this through the story of my personal journey with this work.

I first met Marshall in 1998, at a professional mediation conference in Northern California. I had recently left a graduate program in clinical psychology at Pennsylvania State University and was considering a career in mediation. Having spent years studying how internal conflicts related to psychological health, I was eager to apply what I had learned to people's external conflicts. However, none of the standard approaches to mediation resonated with me. Something was missing, but I didn't know what it was.

There were, however, some things that I did know. As a student, I deeply admired and was passionate about the work of American humanistic psychologist Carl Rogers, who pioneered the application of empathic listening, genuineness, and unconditional positive regard to therapeutic relationships. I was also profoundly inspired by Mahatma Gandhi and the philosophy of nonviolence that he made famous. To my mind, Gandhi was applying similar principles to Rogers, but on a social change level.

More than anything though, I knew that I was drawn to the idea and the experience that all of us are connected to an unfathomable mystery of Life itself, the energy that animates all things and is the source of all. I felt a deep sense of connection, purpose and peace observing nature, entering a place of worship, or even just watching people walking on a city street or riding on a bus. I longed for my work in the world to be connected to that mysterious source and to creating positive social change.

Enter Marshall, who was the keynote speaker at that mediation conference and who impressed me before he ever said a word. The conference organizers were honoring a local mediator for his outstanding service to the community. As the man stood to receive his award, Marshall got up, crossed the stage area, and hugged him. There was something about the way Marshall moved and the warmth of that embrace that told me these two men had deep care and respect for each other. Although I had never seen them before, I felt touched by their interaction.

When Marshall got up on stage, a peculiar stillness fell over the crowd. The atmosphere of the room seemed to hum with an attentive energy as Marshall walked to the podium. On the easel pad, Marshall had sketched two human figures with arrows pointing from the head of each to the heart of the other.

What Marshall said next so perfectly combined everything that I loved in the work of Carl Rogers and Mahatma Gandhi that I could hardly believe it. (I later discovered that Marshall had been Rogers' graduate student.) Marshall talked about a language of the heart, a *language of life*, which connected people to each other and led to "natural giving."

It's part of our basic human nature to want to contribute to one another's well being, Marshall said. As children, we take pleasure in trying to meet another person's needs. But this innate generosity gets crowded out as we learn a language of moralistic judgments, which creep into our interactions. Whether expressed as anger, sarcasm, or passive-aggression, those judgments lead to violence, sometimes physical but more often emotional or psychological.

What I heard Marshall offering through NVC was the ability for human beings to avert destructive conflicts, everywhere. The not-so-secret strategy: To meet conflict compassionately and courageously. The real secret was to do this by practicing a language of human connection. The revelation I heard that day, which I have dedicated my life to transmitting, was that there is a learnable language that can take us into connection and compassion.

In the years that followed, I spent a lot of time with Marshall. Over the next decade, Marshall would often invite me to co-train with him at his nine-day International Intensive Trainings. He and his wife Valentina became close with my family. I learned from him the distinctions we have covered in this volume, but, much more than this, I learned from him to keep bringing my attention and intention back to the purpose of NVC. For him, the purpose was to "create the quality of connection that gets everyone's needs met through compassionate giving and receiving." I could see Marshall modeling this as he worked with people. The look in his eyes, the tone of his voice, and his body language all showed he was connecting with them in a way that was radically different than how I'd seen others listen or relate to people.

Many who have watched Marshall at work describe it as "magic." This may sound like hyperbole, but, I promise you, it's not. When Marshall offered empathy and healing, you didn't see him pausing to think about what words to use, or try to separate observations from evaluations. Certainly he could talk about those distinctions in a teaching context, but when Marshall was empathizing with somebody, *he wasn't thinking about steps or techniques*. He had the ability to directly connect with what was "alive" in this person.

For Marshall, this ability wasn't about thoughts and thinking. One time, I asked him how often he would reflect back people's judgmental thinking when empathizing with them. He said, "John, why would I ever want to focus on what people are thinking? People have been focused on thoughts for thousands of years and look how much suffering and violence has come from them." Marshall wasn't against thinking in and of itself, but he saw what evaluative thinking could do if it wasn't connected to something deeper and wiser within us. He often would say rhetorically, "Why would anyone want their attention on anything other than what's alive in us and what would make life more wonderful?"

What I came to understand was that the NVC language Marshall taught was only a vehicle. What he was really pointing to was something beyond words, something that comes from the willingness to let go of one's limited thinking and connect directly with Life itself, something universal and all pervasive beyond the individual forms. Once in awhile in workshops, and more so in private moments, he would talk about connecting with "Beloved Divine Energy." (He had once referred to it as "Divine Energy," but, after reading the Sufi poets such as Rumi, the experience of a personal relationship with this energy so resonated with him that he added the word "Beloved.") Connecting to his experience of this "energy" was, I believe, the deepest source of what seemed so magical about what Marshall could do when being with people.

At other times, he would talk about how beautiful the energy in people was to him, regardless of how they communicated on the surface. He sometimes used the analogy of riding a surfboard, surfing the life energy in people as he listened intently to them. For Marshall, the language that helped create this connection was feelings and needs, observing what met our needs or didn't, and requesting whatever it was that would meet our needs.

Universal human needs became a core part of NVC language, but this was just a way to structure it for people, a portal to a different consciousness. Of course, a lot of people still try to learn NVC as purely a language technique, which saddened Marshall. *It's about hooking into that energy,* he would insist. *Like a skier getting towed up a hill on the rope pull, you let the energy carry you. Get connected to that energy and the energy does everything else.*

The most radical and moving times I witnessed Marshall extend this idea of life energy and seeing the beauty in people regardless of what they did on the surface was when he would talk about empathizing with people with whom we have "enemy images"—people who act in ways we find disturbing and in ways that violate or transgress our sense of ethics and morality. Marshall went so far as to extend empathy to those who had committed acts of horrific cruelty— to people who raped, murdered, and tortured, including political leaders and dictators who were behind the massive human suffering caused by wars and genocide. Marshall argued that, just like any of us, these people were just human beings who were doing the best they knew to meet their human needs. Tragically, they had not learned how to meet their needs in non-destructive ways. If they had known a better way, wouldn't their choices, and the course of human history, have been different?

Marshall expressed gratitude that he had not learned such destructive strategies in his own life. If he had, Marshall said, he may have developed similar strategies. In workshops, Marshall role-played the part of "villains" with whom it could feel impossible to empathize. He dared to role-play people such as Adolf Hitler, or an African combatant, who, in the midst of an ethnic-religious conflict, had entered a woman's house and killed everyone in her family while she hid under the sink. Through these daring role-plays, Marshall's workshop audiences would be amazed when they began to experience a sense of shared humanity with these people. It was astonishing to suddenly feel heart-wrenching compassion for a person for whom we'd earlier felt nothing but horror and revulsion.

When someone asked Marshall how he could bring himself to play such awful roles and get in touch with our empathy for such people, Marshall would say, "We are all created out of the same energy." He explained that he wasn't just playing those people—he *was* those people—and so are we all. We all have the same human needs. We are all part of the same life force expressing itself through each person.

Marshall had figured out that a language of human needs was an amazingly powerful, effective and practical way to create connection when it's lost. He discovered a language that literally connects us to life itself.

Galvanized as I was by Marshall's language distinctions, I initially found teaching NVC awkward and difficult. While I felt a natural ease in living NVC principles in my own life, it took me some time to figure out how I could best convey those concepts to others.

Then came the chance, in early 2002, to accompany Marshall on that trip to the border of Pakistan to offer conflict resolution training to Afghan tribal elders. Marshall decided to cancel his trip, because the situation was becoming too unstable and dangerous, and the U.S. State Department was warning people not to travel to Pakistan. Crazily, Ike and I decided to go anyway, and the experience cemented both our friendship and our work partnership.

When we got back to the States, we began teaching workshops together on how to apply NVC and mediation to recurring patterns of human conflict and disconnection. And the more workshops we did the more we saw how a "three-chair" mediation framework helped people learn and apply the skills of NVC in their lives, not just in formal mediation contexts. As our body of work grew, our focus shifted. No longer did we aim to teach people only how to mediate external conflicts. (Although we did keep doing that.) It became clear that our three-chair model could apply equally well to internal conflicts and conflicts between ourselves and others, and that resolving internal conflicts could be essential to making forward progress on external ones. We began seeing the importance of focusing on the "fight-flight-freeze" reaction triggered deep in our brains by conflict, and the crucial ingredient of coupling mindfulness-based awareness practices with need consciousness in order to be aware, present, and consciously choose a response to a conflict reaction. A powerful metaphor for this in our training has become to "take the third chair" in any aspect of mediating one's life. We have also developed "maps" to help people overcome deeply ingrained conflict habits, build capacity and resilience, and use their Mediate Your Life skills while in the heat of conflict. By practicing our approach, our participants report that they are creating the lives and relationships they used to only dream about.

It has been interesting for me to look back and see how what Ike and I are doing now brings me full circle, back to that first meeting with Marshall in 1998. In the years that we've developed the Mediate Your Life approach, Ike and I have continually drawn on Marshall's insights. The creativity of our collaborations has been fueled not only by focusing on conflict and combining NVC with a mediation framework, but also by seeing how to integrate in our own way the deeper truths and wisdom laid out by Marshall.

After years of working in the NVC community and with our Mediate Your Life participants, I can tell you that the mediators, coaches, teachers, and leaders who really create transformations for others are those who use the language distinctions, but who also manage to transcend language. Call it a spiritual or meditative approach or whatever you like. The focus on language is secondary. It's in service to a quality of their attention and presence with others.

What I've seen with the advanced participants in our trainings is that all their practice leads to an outward appearance of stillness. As they listen to a practice partner, they're no longer thinking about what to say next. They grow still and quiet and the words just start flowing naturally out of them.

This is what I mean, then, when I say that I hope you eventually "won't need" what you've read in this book. The learning structures we've provided will get you started and will support you in your practice. Then I hope those structures will gradually fall away, as you discover you no longer rely on them, and as you begin to embody a new awareness, and a new way of being in the world.

More and more, Ike and I find that we are not just teaching about conflict resolution. Along with our training participants, we are part of an evolutionary movement toward a new way of being human, one based in awareness and connection that transcends (and includes) thinking that divides and separates.

Mediating conflicts in our daily lives can be about developing awareness by learning to connect with life's connective and creative energies. Ike's story in the front of this book gave a moving example of what becomes possible when we do this. Thanks to Marshall—and thanks to each of you who read this book—we humans really can develop the capacity and skills to bridge our differences, respond together to the challenges we face, and thrive!

Appendix A
Feelings

Feelings are bodily felt experiences and tell us about our needs being met or not met, and about what we are observing, thinking and wanting.

PEACEFUL
tranquil
calm
content
engrossed
absorbed
expansive
serene
loving
blissful
satisfied
relaxed
relieved
quiet
carefree
composed
fulfilled

LOVING
warm
affectionate
tender
appreciative
friendly
sensitive
compassionate
grateful
nurtured
amorous
trusting
open
thankful
radiant
adoring
passionate

GLAD
happy
excited
hopeful
joyful
satisfied
delighted
encouraged
grateful
confident
inspired
touched
proud
exhilarated
ecstatic
optimistic
glorious

PLAYFUL
energetic
effervescent
invigorated
zestful
refreshed
impish
alive
lively
exuberant
giddy
adventurous
mischievous
jubilant
goofy
buoyant
electrified

INTERESTED
involved
inquisitive
intense
enriched
absorbed
alert
aroused
astonished
concerned
curious
eager
enthusiastic
fascinated
intrigued
surprised
helpful

MAD
impatient
pessimistic
disgruntled
frustrated
irritable
edgy
grouchy
agitated
exasperated
disgusted
irked
cantankerous
animosity
bitter
rancorous
irate,furious
angry
hostile
enraged
violent

SAD
lonely
heavy
troubled
helpless
gloomy
overwhelmed
distant
despondent
discouraged
distressed
dismayed
disheartened
despairing
sorrowful
unhappy
depressed
blue
miserable
dejected
melancholy

SCARED
afraid
fearful
terrified
startled
nervous
jittery
horrified
anxious
worried
anguished
lonely
insecure
sensitive
shocked
apprehensive
dread
jealous
desperate
suspicious
frightened

TIRED
exhausted
fatigued
inert
lethargic
indifferent
weary
overwhelmed
fidgety
helpless
heavy
sleepy
disinterested
reluctant
passive
dull
bored
listless
blah
mopey
comatose

CONFUSED
frustrated
perplexed
hesitant
troubled
uncomfortable
withdrawn
apathetic
embarrassed
hurt
uneasy
irritated
suspicious
unsteady
puzzled
restless
boggled
chagrined
unglued
detached
skeptical

For a downloadable and printable version, please visit
http://www.mediateyourlife.com/choosingpeace.

Appendix B
Differentiating Between Feelings And Faux Feelings

These feelings and needs are suggestions only; this listing is neither complete nor definitive. It is intended as an aid to translating words, which are often confused with feelings. These words imply that someone is doing something to you and generally connote wrongness or blame. To use this list: when somebody says "I'm feeling rejected," you might translate this as: "Are you feeling scared because you have a need for inclusion?"

Faux Feeling	Feeling(s)	Need(s)
Abandoned	Terrified, hurt, bewildered, sad, frightened, lonely	Nurturing, connection, belonging, support, caring
Abused	Angry, frustrated, frightened	Caring, nurturing, support, emotional or physical well-being, consideration, need for all living things to flourish
(Not) accepted	Upset, scared, lonely	Inclusion, connection, community, belonging, contribution, peer respect
Attacked	Scared, angry	Safety
Belittled	Angry, frustrated, tense, distressed	Respect, autonomy, to be seen, acknowledgment, appreciation
Betrayed	Angry, hurt, disappointed, enraged	Trust, dependability, honesty, honor, commitment, clarity,

Faux Feeling	Feeling(s)	Need(s)
Blamed	Angry, scared, confused, antagonistic, hostile, bewildered, hurt	Accountability, causality, fairness, justice
Bullied	Angry, scared, pressured	Autonomy, choice, safety, consideration
Caged/ boxed in	Angry, thwarted, scared, anxious	Autonomy, choice, freedom
Cheated	Resentful, hurt, angry	Honesty, fairness, justice, trust, reliability
Coerced	Angry, frustrated, frightened, thwarted, scared	Choice, autonomy, freedom, act freely, choose freely
Cornered	Angry, scared, anxious, thwarted	Autonomy, freedom
Criticized	In pain, scared, anxious, frustrated, humiliated, angry, embarrassed	Understanding, acknowledgement, recognition, accountability, non-judgmental communication
Discounted/ diminished	Hurt, angry, embarrassed, frustrated	Need to matter, acknowledgment, inclusions, recognition, respect
Disliked	Sad, lonely, hurt	Connection, appreciation, understanding acknowledgment, friendship, inclusion
Distrusted	Sad, frustrated	Trust, honesty
Dumped on	Angry, overwhelmed	Respect, consideration

Faux Feeling	Feeling(s)	Need(s)
Harassed	Angry, frustrated, pressured, frightened	Respect, space, consideration, peace
Hassled	Irritated, distressed, angry, frustrated	Serenity, autonomy, do things at my own pace and in my own way, calm, space
Ignored	Lonely, scared, hurt, sad, embarrassed	Connection, belonging, inclusion, community, participation
Insulted	Angry, embarrassed	Respect, consideration, acknowledgment, recognition
Interrupted	Angry, frustrated, resentful, hurt	Respect, to be heard, consideration
Intimidated	Scared, anxiety	Safety, equality, empowerment
Invalidated	Angry, hurt, resentful	Appreciation, respect, acknowledgment, recognition
Invisible	Sad, angry, lonely, scared	To be seen and heard, inclusion, belonging, community
Isolated	Lonely, afraid, scared	Community, inclusion, belonging, contribution
Left out	Sad, lonely, anxious	Inclusion, belonging, community, connection
Let down	Sad, disappointed, frightened	Consistency, trust, dependability
Manipulated	Angry, scared, powerless, thwarted, frustrated	Autonomy, empowerment, trust, equality, freedom, free choice, connection, genuineness
Mistrusted	Sad, angry	Trust

Faux Feeling	Feeling(s)	Need(s)
Misunderstood	Upset, angry, frustrated	To be heard, understanding, clarity
Neglected	Lonely, scared	Connection, inclusion, participation, community, care, mattering, consideration
Overpowered	Angry, impotent, helpless, confused	Equality, justice, autonomy, freedom
Overworked	Angry, tired, frustrated	Respect, consideration, rest, caring
Patronized	Angry, frustrated, resentful	Recognition, equality, respect, mutuality
Pressured	Anxious, resentful, overwhelmed	Relaxation, clarity, space, consideration
Provoked	Angry, frustrated, hostile, antagonistic, resentful	Respect, consideration
Put down	Angry, sad, embarrassed	Respect, acknowledgment, understanding
Rejected	Hurt, scared, angry, defiant	Belonging, inclusion, closeness, to be seen, acknowledgment, connection
Ripped off/ screwed	Anger, resentment, disappointment	Consideration, justice, fairness, justice, acknowledgement, trust
Smothered/ suffocated	Frustrated, fear, desperation	Space, freedom, autonomy, authenticity, self-expression
Taken for granted	Sad, angry, hurt, disappointment	Appreciation, acknowledgment, recognition, consideration

Faux Feeling	Feeling(s)	Need(s)
Threatened	Scared, frightened, alarmed, agitated, defiant	Safety, autonomy
Trampled	Angry, frustrated, overwhelmed	Empowerment, connection, community, being seen, consideration, equality, respect, acknowledgment
Tricked	Embarrassed, angry, resentful	Integrity, trust, honesty
Unappreciated	Sad, angry, hurt, frustrated	Appreciation, respect, acknowledgment, consideration
Unheard	Sad, hostile, frustrated	Understanding, consideration, empathy
Unloved	Sad, bewildered, frustrated	Love, appreciation, empathy, connection, community
Unseen	Sad, anxious, frustrated	Acknowledgment, appreciation, be heard

For a downloadable and printable version, please visit http://www.mediateyourlife.com/choosingpeace.

Appendix C
Universal Human Needs/Values

The needs below are grouped into categories of core needs, 3 meta-categories and 9 subcategories

WELL-BEING

Sustenance/Health	Safety/Security	Beauty/Peace/Play
abundance/thriving	comfort	acceptance
exercise	confidence	appreciation
food/nutrition	emotional safety	gratitude
nourishment	familiarity	awareness
rest/sleep	order	balance
relaxation	structure	ease
shelter	predictability	equanimity
sustainability	protection from harm	humor
support/help	stability	presence
wellness	trust	rejuvenation
vitality	faith	simplicity
energy		space
		tranquility
		wholeness
		wonder

CONNECTION

Love/ Caring	Empathy/ Understanding	Community/ Belonging
affection/warmth	awareness/clarity	cooperation
beauty	acceptance	fellowship
closeness/touch	acknowledgment	generosity
companionship	communication	inclusion
compassion	consideration	interdependence
kindness	hearing (hear/be heard)	harmony/peace
intimacy		hospitality
mattering	knowing (know/be known)	welcoming
importance		mutuality
nurturing	presence/listening	reciprocity
sexual connection	respect/equality	partnership
respect	receptivity/openness	relationship
honoring	recognition	support/solidarity
valuing/prizing	seeing (see/be seen)	trust/dependability
	self-esteem	transparency
	sensitivity	openness

SELF-EXPRESSION

Autonomy/Freedom	Authenticity	Meaning/Contribution
choice	adventure	appreciation/gratitude
clarity	aliveness	achievement
congruence	discovery	productivity
consistency	honesty	celebration/mourning
continuity	initiative	challenge
dignity	innovation	efficacy
freedom	inspiration	effectiveness
independence	joy	excellence
integrity	mystery	growth
power	passion	learning/clarity
empowerment	spontaneity	mystery
self-responsibility		participation
		purpose,/value
		self-actualization
		self-esteem
		skill/mastery

For a downloadable and printable version, please visit
http://www.mediateyourlife.com/choosingpeace.

Appendix D
Putting It All Together

In Chapter 2 we introduced the training wheel sentence, which combines the four components of Observation, Feeling, Need, and Request into one statement. In this Appendix, we explore the training wheel sentence from different perspectives and how to use it in conversation so that you feel more natural. In Appendix E, we give you the basic layout in an easy format to print out to remind you of each part of the sentence.

You'll recall that the structure of this sentence, when focused on yourself, is as follows:

"When I see/hear you _____ [Observation],
I am _____ [Feeling]
because I want _____ [Need];
would you be willing to _____ [Request]?"

The structure is similar when focused on the other person's experience. In that case, the whole sentence becomes the Request, because you are asking the person to tell you what's going on for them and whether your guesses of their Observation, Feelings and Needs are correct:

"When you_____ [Observation],
are you _____ [Feeling]
because you want _____ [Need]?"

Here's an example filled out: (Specifics in bold.)

"When you **start talking while I'm speaking**, are you **excited** because you want **to be heard**?

It's helpful to practice this sentence so you remember it. Then in conversations you can speak more colloquially, so it doesn't sound so much like you are using a particular format. This might mean shifting the components into a different order, using language appropriate for the culture, or even implying one of the components.

Here are a few statements that are more conversational, and their translation into the training wheel format. In a business conversation, you might say:

"I'm really uncertain about this business deal. I'd like some help thinking it through."

As a training wheel sentence, this would be:

"When I **think about this business deal** [Observation], I feel **uncertain** [Feelings] because I need some **help** [Need]."

In the above statement, the request is implicit. If stated explicitly, you could add it to the end as:

"Would you be willing to listen while I talk through my concerns?"

As we noted in Chapter 6 on requests, if you do want something from the person you are speaking with, it's better to state the request rather than leaving it implied. When you leave a request implied, there is always the chance that the other person may be uncertain whether you want something from them.

Here's another daily-life example from your perspective, when you want to let someone else know what's going on for you:

"I'm confused about what we're doing this summer for vacation. Can we talk about it for a few minutes?"

In the above statement, the need is implicit in the feeling of confusion. Generally if we are confused, we need clarity. The request to talk is also stated more conversationally, that is, it is not as specific as it could be. In the training wheel format, with the request stated more specifically, this example would be:

> "When I **think about our summer vacation** [Observation], I feel **confused** [Feeling] because I need **clarity** [Need]; would you be willing to **talk about our plans for ten minutes this afternoon** [Request]?"

When focusing on another person, here's an example in everyday language:

> "Would you like your colleague to get how much work you've put into this, so are you frustrated about what he said in the meeting?"

This sentence turns the order around, starting with Need, then the Feeling, then the Observation. In the training wheel format, it would be:

> "When you **think about what your colleague said in the meeting** [Observation], are you **frustrated** [Feeling] because you'd like **appreciation for your work** [Need], and you would like it from her?"

Notice that, again, since you are asking the other person to respond to your guesses as to what is going on for them, these are examples where the entire sentence is the request. Here's another example in everyday language focusing on what is going on for the other person:

> "Are you bummed about the phone call because you'd like to get along with your mom better?"

Notice that the need in both this and the previous example is expressed informally. Recall that a need as we mean it in this work is not tied to a particular person, place, or thing (see

Chapter 5), so stating a need this way would more likely be an initial guess, and as you continue empathizing with the person, your next statement might distance the need from the mom.

In the training wheel format, the above question would sound like:

> "When you **think about the phone call with your mother** [Observation], are you **discouraged** [Feeling] because you want **connection** [Need], and you'd really like it with her?

You might even combine both your own perspective and the other person's into a colloquial statement, since that is how we naturally speak:

> "I'm reluctant to go to your office holiday party since I've got so much on my plate already; are you hoping that your going will bring you closer together with your colleagues?

Rephrased as training wheel sentences, these might be divided into two sentences, one for attention on you and one for attention on the other person:

> "When I **think about going to your holiday party** [Observation], I feel **reluctant** [Feeling] because I need **rest** [Need],"

–and–

> "When you **consider going to the holiday party** [Observation], are you feeling **enthused** [Feeling] because **of the sense of belonging it would give you** [Need]?"

Often, these will be split into multiple exchanges, perhaps empathizing with the other person first and then expressing your feelings and needs. However, if you are eager to be heard, you can express yourself first, and then ask immediately about what's motivating the other person. When you do so, you give yourself a bit of empathy because you've connected with your own need. Then try to connect with what is going on for the other person. This approach is more likely to keep the conversation going than if you only state that you don't want to go to the party.

As you can probably tell, in comparison to the conversational examples, the training wheel sentence can sound formal and even stilted. Though the training wheel sentence can definitely be used in some cases, it is likely to seem a departure from how we normally speak. It also may contain too much information, particularly if you are focused on what is going on for the other person. If you have to guess at more than one of the components, it's better to focus in on those components one at a time rather than throw a bunch of guesses into one statement. Thus, often in empathizing with someone else, we tend to focus on one or maybe two components at a time, rather than all of them at once, and build up to all four if the situation warrants. We can keep the training wheel sentence in mind to support us in remembering and tracking whether we have clarity about the components that seem important in any given moment.

In the techniques of the previous chapters, we mostly gave examples of just one interchange between your partner and you, however, conversations are rarely so neat and tidy. It might take several exchanges between you and the other person to hone in on any one of the components. For example, let's say your friend Fred says to you, "I need a car." You might respond first with "You want a car?" Fred exclaims, "Yes, a red sports car!" Then you might guess the need by saying, "So, are you looking for fun?" Fred replies, "Well, sort of, girls mainly."

Then you might clarify the need by asking, "Is it that you would like a car for more romance in your life?" Or, "Oh, so a car like that might get you more dates?"

Now, if instead of saying, "Yes, a red sports car," let's say Fred replied, "Yes, a seven passenger minivan!" then you would be in a different conversation with different needs. The red roadster may have been the car desired a few years earlier, prior to shuttling a pack of kids to soccer practice and basketball games.

Talking things out helps people get more clear on what happened, how they feel about it, what their needs are, and what they would like—their requests. Your back and forth with them can be an invaluable part of the process of achieving clarity for both of you, thus creating more connection between you.

MOMENT-BY-MOMENT CHOICE: USING THE FOUR COMPONENTS IN REAL-LIFE SITUATIONS

In each moment of a conversation, we make a choice about what to do (i.e., reflect, express ourselves, empathize with the other person, make a request, connect internally with our own needs, etc.), do it, and then move on to the next choice. We can think of the 4 Components of Observation, Feelings, Needs, and Requests as well as the techniques in the previous chapters as the toolbox from which we are choosing in our communication with others, and with ourselves. At every step we make a judgment call about what we will say; will we choose to reflect, or guess someone's needs? Will we focus on clarifying the other person's request, or expressing our own needs? At this point, the options might seem overwhelming; after all, we just finished presenting seventeen different techniques! How do you decide what to do in the moment?

First, remember that the intention behind using this language is to connect with the other person. The choices you make will ultimately go back to what you think will be most likely to create that connection. From our experience in our work, and also via the trainings where we've taught hundreds of people how to use these tools, there are a few things we can say about what we have found creates connection. However, every situation and person is different, and your task is to find out what works for you. This happens through practice and experience.

Second, to make these choices it helps to be clear what the purpose is in the conversation; you will make different choices depending on whether you are there to simply be with the person, or to give them feedback, offer advice, or to elicit information from them. The purpose might change throughout the conversation, but at every moment your purpose can serve as a guide to the choices you make.

Third, it can help to recall that each component has its place in communication designed to connect rather than create division. We talk about needs as being the most connecting because they are the universal translators. Regardless of the situation, they help you know what is motivating another person in a way that you can directly relate to your own experience. They similarly help someone else know what is going on for you so they can relate to your experience. The other components have their purpose too. Sharing observations orients the conversation, indicating what you are talking about, and can sometimes be helpful as the context for the need. Noticing feelings highlights the emotional response to what has happened, and points to the universal human needs that are or are not being met by what happened. Requests take all the other components and put them into action, stating what you would like to happen in the world. Remembering how each component helps you connect can support making choices in a conversation.

When you stay curious and connected when communicating with someone, you'll find that we all have our own answers. You may to need to come to your own answers in your own way in order to live them in the world. When in conversation, you can continue simply asking questions to help clarify the Observations, Feelings, Needs, and Requests, trusting that by being present and empathetic, you are helping the person find their own answers in their own way.

This is why we think of a conversation where we are providing empathy as a conversation in which we are following instead of leading. Assume the other person has the answers, and let go of attachment to your own guesses. The first guess is like the first homemade pancake—it's not necessarily on the mark. You don't want to be attached to that guess; you want to shift to whatever correction or clarification the person gives. Go with what they say is true for them.

When empathizing with another person, every response you make is a judgment call. You do not know how someone will respond to a particular statement, you can only be clear about your intention and what you say or do. If you are clear that your intention is to support, understand, or contribute, then you can choose from any of the techniques we've talked about in the previous chapters to do that. Let the other person lead the conversation, and follow them, reflecting back and clarifying their Observations, Feelings, Needs and Requests as you go.

Appendix E
Expressing Compassionately

1. Guess the observable behavior.

When I
$\left\{\begin{array}{l}\text{see} \\ \text{hear} \\ \text{remember} \\ \text{imagine}\end{array}\right\}$ _____

2. Express my feelings.

I feel _____

_____

3. Communicate my need/preference.

Because I would have liked _____

_____

Because I was
$\left\{\begin{array}{l}\text{needing} \\ \text{hoping} \\ \text{wanting}\end{array}\right\}$ _____

4. Make a request in positive action language.
And right now, would you be willing to:
   a. tell me what you heard me say;
   b. tell me how you feel about what you heard me say;
   c. tell me if you would be willing to _____

Receiving Empathically

1. Identify the observable behavior.

When you $\left\{\begin{array}{l}\text{see}\\\text{hear}\\\text{remember}\\\text{imagine}\end{array}\right\}$ _____

—OR—

Are you reacting to
Are you talking about $\left.\right\}$ _____
Are you referring to

2. Guess the feelings.

Are you feeling
I'm guessing you're feeling $\left.\right\}$ _____

3. Guess the unmet need/preference.

Because you would have liked $\left.\right\}$ _____
Because you were needing

4. Guess what the request might be.

So now, are you wanting
And now, would you like me to $\left.\right\}$ _____

For a downloadable and printable version, please visit
http://www.mediateyourlife.com/choosingpeace.

Appendix F
About the Authors

Both authors have extensive experience in work with conflict and mediating conflict. Here is more about the authors in their own words:

IKE LASATER:

I was a trial lawyer in San Francisco, trying larger and larger civil cases over the course of twenty years. I saw the limitations of the law for resolving disputes. American law evolved from English Common Law. One of the key motivations for the early development of English Common Law, particularly the jury system, was the kings' desire for a process that would resolve disputes among their subjects, and to resolve them in a way that would prevent their subjects from resorting to feuds. Resolution was emphasized over the satisfaction of the parties. Modern law has the same focus. In my work, I saw so much wasted effort in litigation; generally people didn't talk seriously about settling claims until close to a trial date, when people were pushed up against the uncertainty of the result, which might be years into the lawsuit.

I was unimpressed by the mediation I experienced in settlement conferences; usually it involved shuttle diplomacy, where the parties were in different rooms and the mediator would carry proposals back and forth. Mediators used various techniques to stimulate fear in people, focusing on the risks of not reaching settlement to force an agreement. This was useful in the sense that the parties might reach an agreement, but I do not recall anyone enjoying the process, and it certainly didn't occur to me that healing could result from mediation. The common wisdom in traditional mediation is that both parties should be equally pissed off with the result of the mediation, as that indicates a fair compromise.

At the same time I was dissatisfied with the way disputes were resolved in the courts, I was also struggling with conflicts in my own life. I was a founding partner in a law firm, and we had nearly twenty people working for us. People would get into conflict, and those conflicts would disrupt the entire staff for a few weeks. Whenever I as a manager tried to get those in conflict together, I felt like I'd thrown gasoline on the fire. I felt helpless to deal with these situations, as well as the conflicts that I experienced with my family.

During the last four or five years of my law career, I was actively looking for consultants to deal with conflicts. That was when I stumbled across Marshall Rosenberg's work. I went to a small workshop he did in San Francisco in 1996. Less than an hour into the workshop, I understood all the words but realized something was going on that I didn't grok, but wanted to. I was hooked: I had found a life-affirming way to communicate what was important between people. I continued my learning with NVC and, because I was so impressed with the impact that NVC could have, I accepted Marshall's request to join the Center for Nonviolent Communication Board in 1999. I served on the board for six years.

JOHN KINYON:

I was trained as a clinical psychologist but wasn't sure how I wanted to contribute to the world. My passion for psychology was always about conflict, how we get disconnected from ourselves and others, and how can we be present and listen in a way that is healing and transformative. My main question was: How do we go from conflict to connection, either on a personal level with each other, or on a social level of maintaining human connection in the midst of social conflict and change?

I felt very drawn to the work of psychologist Carl Rogers and to Gandhi's philosophy and practice of nonviolence, and was looking for something to do that would bring my interests together. I thought mediation might be one way to do this. I went to a day-long mediation conference in 1998, and Marshall Rosenberg was the keynote speaker. About a minute into his talk, I had the experience of clouds parting. I saw clearly how Nonviolent Communication brought together these interests in a way I never imagined was possible.

I started attending NVC trainings and eventually co-founded BayNVC (the San Francisco Bay Area affiliate of the Center for Nonviolent Communication), became a trainer, and joined the Center for Nonviolent Communication board of directors. I met Ike while on the CNVC board, but really, as we shared earlier, our experience in Pakistan created the bond between us.

Appendix G
About The Training

MEDIATE YOUR LIFE PROGRAMS

We offer a variety of different types of training and ways to access our work. Our flagship program is our immersion program, which consists of three four-day retreats spread out over the course of about nine months, with practice requests between each workshop. These retreats build on each other, but you can take each as a stand-alone workshop and do them in any order. We are now also offering this program in a teleclass version through the NVC Academy.

We also offer 2- to 3-day workshops on a variety of topics that relate to navigating and resolving conflicts. These workshops are a great way to sample our work and get support on specific areas where you might experience conflict. Topics include:

- Having Difficult Conversations
- Resolving Conflicts from the Inside Out
- Getting Unstuck from Indecision, Guilt, and Shame
- Change Your Habitual Response to Conflict
- Making Amends: Healing and Reconciling
  Emotional Hurt

See our website at MediateYourLife.com to find out more about any of our programs.

WHO OUR WORK HELPS

We've worked with a variety of people in our trainings over the last ten years. We've worked with men and women, ranging from their 20s to their 60s. We have worked with people in a variety of professions, including lawyers, business people, university administrators, mediators, educators, community relations specialists, coaches, and therapists. Our workshop participants often have made significant accomplishments already in their communities, families, or workplace, but these accomplishments are either not fully seen, or not sufficiently satisfying. They are seeking more depth, more of, as the Pulitzer Prize winning poet Mary Oliver calls it, "this one wild and precious life."

BENEFITS OF MEDIATE YOUR LIFE TRAININGS

"[The training] increased my hope for the future."
-Immersion Program Graduate

The graduates of our Mediate Your Life trainings have told us they experience more ease and compassion with themselves. They are able to listen with more focus and without becoming defensive. They report improved relationships with the key people in their lives: their work colleagues, intimate partner, parents, and children. As one participant told us, in speaking about improving her relationship with her parents, "I can better understand, reflect and hold their needs, and I am also more empowered to assert my needs. The result is that I feel significantly closer and more open to both of my parents—no small feat!"

In our trainings, people report improvements in their ability to handle conflict situations in their lives. As one participant said, "As a result of taking this training I am confronting conflicts with friends and people I care most about sooner and with a higher degree of calm and equanimity than ever before."

Another participant in our year-long program said, "When I came to the training, I still felt quite a bit of nervousness around conflict, yet also felt that conflict was rich in possibility for deeper connection. I was hopeful that the training would allow me to mine this depth. Also, I yearned for skills and competence. I wanted to have the tools that would allow me to stand in the fire of conflict without being burned. What I have experienced in the past year is all that and more. A few of the most important things I have gained include: a ready ability to self-connect and the awareness to remember to do so, a trust in my ability to be with whatever shows up, the realization that for me almost every strategy I employ is at its core an attempt to experience self-acceptance... at least at this time in my life, that's what it all boils down to. Somehow knowing this about myself gives me a sense of compassion for myself that I lacked before."

This connection to self is another important result people report, and accompanies a sense of being better able to act in a way that feels authentic. As another participant wrote, "The most useful tool I gained from the training was learning how to stay self-connected and present with my internal and interpersonal conflicts. This all-important tool has opened up the space for me to truly listen to my heart, listen with my heart, and act in a manner that is true to myself and to others. I have always longed to be in this space of love and connection and am elated to have gained this ability."

Others experience a wide range of positive results that impact every area of their lives. Here are some reports from our trainings:

"I am more engaged, more open, less afraid, more focused, more clear about what I want to do, happier and more able to connect with myself and everyone else, [and] happier and more able to contribute to the connections and happiness of other people."

"The reality is that every aspect of my life has been changed for the better. Most importantly I now know that when I remain present and listen to myself and to the people that come in and out of my life with my heart wide open beautiful things happen."

And, ultimately, all of this leads to experiencing more peace, joy, and hope in life, as this one participant shared: "I am experiencing more and more peace in myself, dealing with internal conflict in ways that are immensely healing. I am working more from a quiet joy, rather than anxiety."

Appendix H
Resources

Duhigg, Charles. *The Power of Habit: Why We Do What We Do in Life and Business.* New York: Random House, 2012. Print.

Eagleman, David. Incognito: *The Secret Lives of the Brain.* New York: Pantheon Books, a division of Random House, Inc., 2011. Print

Ekman, Paul. *Emotions Revealed: Recognizing Faces and Feelings to Improve Communication and Emotional Life.* 2nd Edition. New York: Holt Paperbacks, 2007. Print.

Frankl, Viktor E. *Man's Search for Meaning.* New York: Simon & Schuster, 1984. Print.

Gazzaniga, Michael. *Who's in Charge?: Free Will and the Science of the Brain.* New York: HarperCollins, 2011. Print.

Kahneman, Daniel. *Thinking, Fast and Slow.* New York: Farrar, Straus, and Giroux, 2011. Print.

Kenrick, Douglas T. and Griskevicius, Vladas. *The Rational Animal: How Evolution Made Us Smarter Than We Think.* New York: Basic Books, 2013. Print.

Lasater, Ike with Julie Stiles. *Words That Work in Business: A Practical Guide to Effective Communication in the Workplace.* Encinitas, CA: PuddleDancer Press, 2010. Print.

Lasater, Judith Hanson and Ike Lasater. *What We Say Matters: Practicing Nonviolent Communication.* Berkeley, CA: Rodmell Press, 2009. Print.

McGonigal, Kelly. *The Willpower Instinct: How Self-Control Works, Why It Matters, and What You Can Do To Get More of It.* New York: The Penguin Group, 2012. Print.

Rosenberg, Marshall B. *Nonviolent Communication: A Language of Compassion.* Encinitas, CA: PuddleDancer Press, 1999. Print.

Sapolsky, Robert M. *Why Zebras Don't Have Ulcers (3rd ed.).* New York: Holt Paperbacks, 2004. Print.

Stress: Portrait of a Killer. Dir. John Heminway. 2008. National Geographic Television & Stanford University. DVD.

Vedantam, Shankar. *The Hidden Brain: How Our Unconscious Minds Elect Presidents, Control Markets, Wage Wars, and Save Our Lives.* New York: Spiegel & Grau and imprint of the Random House Publishing Group, a division of Random House, Inc. 2010.